Digital Dilemmas

Øyvind Kvalnes
Digital Dilemmas
Exploring Social Media Ethics in Organizations

Øyvind Kvalnes
Department of Leadership and Organizational Behaviour
BI Norwegian Business School
Oslo, Norway

ISBN 978-3-030-45926-0   ISBN 978-3-030-45927-7 (eBook)
https://doi.org/10.1007/978-3-030-45927-7

© The Editor(s) (if applicable) and The Author(s) 2020. This book is an open access publication.
Open Access This book is licensed under the terms of the Creative Commons Attribution 4.0 International License (http://creativecommons.org/licenses/by/4.0/), which permits use, sharing, adaptation, distribution and reproduction in any medium or format, as long as you give appropriate credit to the original author(s) and the source, provide a link to the Creative Commons licence and indicate if changes were made.

The images or other third party material in this book are included in the book's Creative Commons licence, unless indicated otherwise in a credit line to the material. If material is not included in the book's Creative Commons licence and your intended use is not permitted by statutory regulation or exceeds the permitted use, you will need to obtain permission directly from the copyright holder.

The use of general descriptive names, registered names, trademarks, service marks, etc. in this publication does not imply, even in the absence of a specific statement, that such names are exempt from the relevant protective laws and regulations and therefore free for general use.

The publisher, the authors and the editors are safe to assume that the advice and information in this book are believed to be true and accurate at the date of publication. Neither the publisher nor the authors or the editors give a warranty, expressed or implied, with respect to the material contained herein or for any errors or omissions that may have been made. The publisher remains neutral with regard to jurisdictional claims in published maps and institutional affiliations.

Cover pattern: © Melisa Hasan

This Palgrave Macmillan imprint is published by the registered company Springer Nature Switzerland AG.
The registered company address is: Gewerbestrasse 11, 6330 Cham, Switzerland

Acknowledgments

I wrote this book while on sabbatical from my job at BI Norwegian Business School in the autumn of 2019. Most of it was written during my research stays at Reykjavik University and Aalto University, Helsinki. I would like to thank my colleagues and friends in those places for their support and encouragement. Special mention goes to Kaffihús Vesturbæjar in Reykjavik for being an excellent place to work. I am grateful to my colleague Arne Carlsen for his valuable input to an early draft of the manuscript. I thank my employer BI Norwegian Business School for funding the book and for making it possible to publish it with Open Access. Finally, a warm thank you to the executive students who provided the digital dilemmas on which I have built the categorization in this book.

Contents

1 Digital Dilemmas in Organizations — 1
   1 Ethics on Social Media — 4
   2 Morality, Ethics and Dilemmas — 6
   3 Methodology — 8
   References — 12

2 Dilemmas in Social Media: A Categorization — 17
   1 Role Dilemmas — 19
   2 Tempo Dilemmas — 23
   3 Integrity Dilemmas — 26
   4 Speech Dilemmas — 30
   5 Competence Dilemmas — 34
   6 A Spectrum of Dilemmas — 36
   References — 40

3 Ethical Navigation on Social Media — 43
   1 A Speech Dilemma — 45
   2 Principle of Equality — 49
   3 Principle of Publicity — 52
   4 The Navigation Wheel — 54
   5 Ethical Debriefing — 58
   References — 62

4 Leadership and Ethics in Social Media 65
   1   Ethical Leadership 68
   2   Balanced Leadership 73
   3   Doing Good and Avoiding Harm 76
   References 80

Index 83

List of Figures

Fig. 2.1   Spectrum of dilemmas   39
Fig. 3.1   The Navigation Wheel. (Source: Kvalnes, Ø., & Øverenget, E. (2012). Ethical navigation in leadership training. *Etikk i praksis—Nordic Journal of Applied Ethics* 6(1), 58–71)   55

List of Tables

Table 2.1   Categories of dilemmas   19
Table 4.1   Do-good and avoid-harm ethics issues in social media   77

1

Digital Dilemmas in Organizations

Abstract Social media platforms are at the core of the digital transformation of organizations. This chapter outlines the current study's threefold purpose, which is to (1) categorize ethical dilemmas that can occur for professionals who run social media platforms for their organizations, (2) propose conceptual tools for reflecting on those dilemmas and (3) outline how social media ethics affects leadership in organizations. Social media enables individuals, groups and organizations to publish content without going through an editor, so it facilitates quick exchanges with a range of stakeholders. The current study is the first to map and categorize the ethical dilemmas that can occur in organizations that use social media. Input for the study comes from executive students at a European business school. The study's overall aim is to provide a platform for systematic and reflective handling of ethical dilemmas for practitioners who are responsible for social media accounts at their organizations.

Keywords Ethical dilemmas • Social media • Organizational ethics • Facebook • Leadership

Anne is a communications advisor for a construction company. One of her tasks is to run a Facebook account dedicated to a construction project in the mountains, where the company is building a large tunnel. The construction manager is a good photographer, and he frequently submits photos from the project for publication on Facebook. People can follow the progress and milestones of the tunnel construction through its Facebook account. This creates pride in and excitement about the project, and the employees are energized by such frequent public displays of their achievements. One day, Anne receives a new set of photos from the construction manager and immediately posts them on Facebook. This time, one photo happens to document a serious health, safety and environment (HSE) violation by one of the employees. The purpose of posting the photo was to document normal activity at the project, but it shows a worker in action without a helmet. The company has recently had serious accidents at the project site due to a lack of helmet use. Angry users have already noted the violation and commented about it on Facebook. How should Anne cope with the situation? Either she can respond to the criticism and risk bringing even more attention to the HSE violation, or she can delete the photo and hope that there will be no further criticism. No matter what she decides to do, there is a risk of subsequent problems.

Social media platforms are at the core of digital transformations in organizations. They introduce a range of new ways for individuals, groups and organizations to spread, share and comment on ideas, beliefs and information (Kane, 2017; Kaplan & Haenlein, 2010). People no longer need to go through an editor to publish their opinions or photos to a wide audience. Exchanges happen quickly, creating a sense of always being current and up to date. This fast tempo also increases the risk of mistakes, as in the example involving Anne and the publication of a photo documenting an HSE violation. The combination of an increased scope of action and rapid publication creates a range of ethical dilemmas for decision-makers within organizations. Those who are responsible for handling organizations' social media accounts can face situations in which they must prioritize conflicting ethical considerations. No matter what they decide to do, something of ethical value is lost.

This book is aimed at categorizing the concrete digital dilemmas that occur when organizations use social media platforms to interact with stakeholders. Data were collected from approximately 250 executive students at a European business school over a five-year period. Each student was invited to formulate a personal digital dilemma, a situation at work in which they had to prioritize certain ethical considerations. The students are practitioners responsible for handling social media platforms for their organizations. As such, they have first-hand experience with encountering and addressing ethical challenges related to organizational social media use.

The book has a threefold purpose. First, it sets out to categorize ethical dilemmas that arise for people who handle social media platforms for organizations across industries, disciplines and professions. No previous studies have aimed to accomplish this goal. Research on the ethical aspects of social media use tends to be industry and discipline specific. The current study contributes to a much-needed clarification of the concrete dilemmas that arise in workplaces adapting to a reality in which social media platforms have created a radically different environment for conversation and interaction. The author previously outlined this categorization in a book chapter (Kvalnes, 2019), but this book contains the first detailed account.

Second, the book provides a systematic framework for analyzing ethical dilemmas related to social media use. A key component of this framework is the Navigation Wheel developed by Kvalnes and Øverenget (2012). It guides decision-makers through a process of considering questions regarding law (is it legal?), identity (is it in accordance with our corporate or professional values?), morality (is it in line with our convictions and beliefs about right and wrong?), reputation (does it affect our goodwill?), economy (is it profitable?) and ethics (can we justify it using ethical principles and theories?). The Navigation Wheel framework can be used in teaching and learning processes in academic and other organizational settings.

Third, the book addresses how digital dilemmas and ethics on social media have consequences for leadership. Many of this study's informants reported weak or absent support from their leaders when dealing with such dilemmas. In some cases, the leaders even pushed the responsibility of responding to ethically questionable uses of social media in the organization onto employees who are social media experts rather than doing it themselves. The book analyzes these tendencies and their possible remedies under the headings of ethical leadership (Brown, Treviño, & Harrison, 2005) and balanced leadership (Müller, Packendorff, & Sankaran, 2017).

1 Ethics on Social Media

Social media has been defined as "a group of Internet-based applications that build on the ideological and technological foundations of Web 2.0, and allow the creation and exchange of user generated content" (Kaplan & Haenlein, 2010, p. 61). It can be seen as a diverse and evolving technological infrastructure that supports and changes how people communicate and collaborate (Kane, 2017). Facebook, Twitter, LinkedIn, Snapchat and other social media platforms create a multitude of ways an organization can develop and disseminate its corporate identity (Devereux, Melewar, & Foroudi, 2017). Inappropriate social media strategies can rapidly create and fuel corporate crises (Ott & Theunissen, 2015).

Social media creates ethical challenges that go beyond those addressed in traditional media ethics, which positions the professional editor as the prime decision-maker (Kieran, 2002) and concerns itself with the duties of journalists before, during and after publication (Bertrand, 2018; Duffy & Knight, 2019). Social media enables individuals to be their own publishers, and this creates new and unfamiliar ethical dilemmas for practitioners in the field. This book attempts to identify and address such dilemmas in a systematic manner with the dual ambition of contributing to organizational ethics research and offering a conceptual framework to ease the ethical tension that practitioners experience through the categorization and through the framework for ethical analysis.

The decision-makers in traditional media are journalists and editors, who are responsible for the content they publish. Information that reaches the public through various media shapes people's worldviews, perceptions and attitudes, placing a particularly strong ethical responsibility on the professionals who decide what to publish and how to publicize it (Kieran, 2002). Journalists are expected to follow ethical guidelines and principles that reflect their power to influence people's mindsets (Ward, 2005). As professionals, they have a particular responsibility to remain honest and act in the public interest (Iggers, 2018). Digital journalists face a range of complex ethical challenges in relation to misinformation and fake news (Bakir & McStay, 2018; Lazer et al., 2018; Pennycook & Rand, 2019).

Users of Facebook, Twitter, Instagram, LinkedIn, Snapchat and other social media platforms are their own publicists. They do not depend on the support of an editor or a journalist to make their content publicly available. Traditional media ethics fail to the range of ethical issues that arise under these radically changed communication conditions. Social media users can play multiple roles and serve multiple purposes that go far beyond those of an editor or a journalist. They, too, may have strong reasons to be concerned about honesty, the public interest and the reliability of information, but their scope of action is wider and less restricted by professional norms, duties and expectations.

The thrills of social media use include the rapid exchange of ideas and the impulsive posting of content. However, this fast tempo also creates ethical problems. The opening example from the construction company illustrates how carefree and immediate social media use creates dilemmas for decision-makers. Two mistakes have already occurred. The first was the employee's HSE violation of working in an unsafe environment without a helmet, and the second was to publish a photo documenting that mistake on Facebook. Now the person responsible for company's social media accounts must determine how to deal with the situation. None of the options available to her is without ethical costs. In the name of transparency and honesty, she can reply to the critic, then remove the photo. In the name of protecting the employee and the organization from further public scrutiny for the mistake, she can remove the photo immediately and proceed with the hope that viewers will move on and make no further comments about it. There are no harmonious options available in which everyone is satisfied with the ethical aspects of the decision. This example is presented and discussed in further detail in Chap. 3.

2 Morality, Ethics and Dilemmas

Kahneman (2013) distinguished between two modes of decision-making. System 1 is his name for the quick, intuitive mode, whereas System 2 is his label for the slow, analytic mode. This distinction is relevant in the current context of investigating dilemmas related to social media. When challenging situations occur, decision-makers can decide and act intuitively based on gut feelings about what they should do under such circumstances, or they can take time to think through the available options, consider their advantages and disadvantages in light of how they affect different stakeholders and reach a decision.

We can bring the concepts of morality and ethics into play to describe these decision-making processes. Morality can be understood as people's personal and shared beliefs about right and wrong. These beliefs develop over time in social settings because people develop moral standards and convictions through social learning processes. Ethics, on the other hand, can be defined as the academic discipline of thinking systematically about right and wrong (Goodpaster, 1992; Kvalnes, 2019). People can learn ethics from reading books and attending courses and seminars. Ethical principles and theories can guide our reasoning about right and wrong. For example, the Golden Rule is an ethical principle situated in various religious and nonreligious traditions that serves as an action-guiding tool for decision-makers.

With these definitions of morality and ethics in place, we can distinguish between two ways of reaching a decision in a dilemma. The first is to apply moral intuition and quickly determine a course of action (System 1), and the second is to slow down and apply ethical theories and principles to the case at hand (System 2). Chapter 3 presents a set of principles that can guide decision-making in social media contexts. The Navigation Wheel is a cognitive tool that provides a framework for analyzing ethical dilemmas. It can also be applied in situations outside that context, so it is not uniquely designed for handling ethical dilemmas on social media.

Egorov, Verdorfer, and Peus (2018) argued against a rationalistic tendency in studies of ethical decision-making in organizations and claimed that moral intuition plays an unacknowledged and significant role in those processes. The current exploration of digital dilemmas and ethics in the context of social media does not deny the relevance of quick moral thinking, but is concerned with its limitations. The proposed systematic tools for handling dilemmas supplement moral intuitions rather than downgrade them, so using these tools does not constitute overt rationalism in the sense described by Egorov et al. (2018).

A dilemma can be defined as a situation in which the decision-maker must choose between two or more alternatives that have more or less equal moral weight or ethical value (Kvalnes, 2019; Maclagan, 2003, 2012). No matter what he or she decides to do, one or more important consideration must be prioritized at the expense of another. Thus, whatever the agent decides to do, there will be an element of wrongness to it (Brinkmann, 2005; Kvalnes, 2019; Maclagan, 2003, 2012; Toffler, 1986). It is common to distinguish between dilemmas and temptations (Brinkmann, 2005), or between real and false dilemmas (Kvalnes, 2019; Maclagan, 2003, 2012). The former are situations in which there is a genuine tension between two or more alternatives that have a strong moral or ethical value attached to them, and it is difficult to identify the best alternative. The latter are situations in which it is rather obvious what one should do, from an ethical perspective, but one is tempted, ordered or for other reasons drawn toward the unethical alternative.

Previous studies have focused on industry-specific ethical dilemmas and challenges related to the uses of social media. In medicine, there is an emerging awareness of the ethical implications of social media use that involves sharing stories and pictures of patients (McKlindon et al., 2016; Palacios-González, 2015; Wells, Lehavot, & Isaac, 2015). Warnick, Bitters, Falk, and Kim (2016) discussed the responsibilities of teachers who interact with their pupils or students on social media, and Fenwick (2016) suggested that responsible use of social media should be an integral element of teaching professionalism to students. An emerging research stream focuses on the use of social media to collect big data for research, product development and marketing. Social media can vastly improve the reach and efficiency of such processes, but the available methods also create considerable ethical dilemmas with regard to privacy

(Bender, Cyr, Arbuckle, & Ferris, 2017; Gelinas et al., 2017; Kosinski, Matz, Gosling, Popov, & Stillwell, 2015; Mittelstadt & Floridi, 2016).

The novelty of the current study is that it identifies generic ethical dilemmas that can occur across industries and sectors. Such dilemmas can arise in any organization that uses social media to communicate with its stakeholders. The findings and discussion are thus relevant in any organization that uses social media.

3 Methodology

Executive students at a European business school provided input for the present categorization of ethical dilemmas. The students participated in a Master of Management program on digitalization and leadership. The program included five 4-day modules and ran from September to May. The students are professionals aged 30 and above in the private and public sectors. They work with the implementation of digital platforms and social media strategies and practices at their own organizations.

In four of the five modules, the students participated in a three-hour ethics session in which they became familiar with ethical concepts and theories and applied them in discussions of concrete cases. The author of this book was their teacher for all modules. In the period between modules 1 and 2 (four to six weeks), the students completed a home assignment titled "My digital dilemma" that consisted of writing up one ethical dilemma connected to their own experiences using social media at work. The data for the current study are derived from the memos the students handed in for this assignment. The data were collected from classes of around 50 students during each study year from 2013–2014 to 2017–2018. Thus, approximately 250 students contributed to the data set through their participation in the assignment.

Dilemmas submitted by the students were also used during teaching sessions, and that process generated new examples that were outlined orally in the classroom by students who were reminded of similar episodes from their own organizations and work environments.

The threefold motivation behind the home assignment of describing a social media dilemma was as follows:

1. Stimulate the students' ethical self-reflection by encouraging them to explore the connections between ethical concepts and their own work practices.
2. Generate a social media dilemma bank for use when teaching future classes in the same program.
3. Investigate and research what executive students consider the main ethical challenges of social media use in their organizations.

The students consented to the anonymized use of their contributions. Whenever a dilemma was considered for use in a teaching module for which the contributor would be present, that person was asked (1) for permission to use the dilemma in that context and (2) whether he or she wanted to be anonymous or open about being the source of the dilemma. In the latter case, the student could then elaborate on further details and discuss the dilemma with the teacher and fellow students. Whenever a dilemma has been considered for quotation, the student who provided it was given the opportunity to withdraw it or request revisions to ensure anonymization. No students chose to withdraw their contribution, but one asked for further anonymization before accepting the inclusion of her dilemma in this book.

The assignment proceeded from the dilemma definition provided above but highlighted that students needed not describe a dilemma in its strictest form. Maclagan (2003) noted that actual dilemma cases tend to occur on a spectrum between what people perceive as real and false dilemmas. On one side of the scale are real dilemmas in their purest form, in which people perceive the ethical weight of both alternatives as equal. On the other side of the scale are false dilemmas, in which one option is clearly ethically optimal, while the other is obviously unethical, but the decision-maker is nevertheless drawn to the unethical choice because he or she is tempted or under pressure to perform it. Most cases in the material used in this study are not so clear. In addition, people disagree about the ethical weight of the available alternatives and, therefore, the extent to which they are real or false dilemmas. However, all the cases are ethically challenging because they test the decision-maker's ability to weigh ethical values and other considerations against each other.

The dilemma outlined at the beginning of this chapter belongs to the side of the scale closest to that of the false dilemmas. It might be tempting to remove the photo and hope that the publicized HSE violation goes more or less unnoticed and that the critic calms down, but from an ethical perspective, the organization should most likely acknowledge the mistake and publish a reply to the critic before removing the photo. The employee who made the mistake might prefer the option to immediately remove the photo, but the ethical weight of shielding him and the organization from further public scrutiny and criticism is less than that of being transparent and open about the mistake.

The opening dilemma was described in a memo written by one of the student informants. The material overall is multifaceted and rich, and it illustrates the ethical challenges and confusion that can arise with the emergence of new technology. The students signaled that it is difficult to cope with these situations at work because of the following:

1. Insufficient support from leaders, who tend to have a restricted understanding of how social media works
2. A lack of established codes or norms
3. An absence of narratives about exemplary handlings of previous cases
4. Limited access to concepts and ideas that clarify the issues at stake

Initial meetings with these students highlighted a need for research to elucidate the ethical challenges they encounter at work. The current book sets out to provide this by providing a systematic account of the ethical dilemmas that can arise for employees who handle social media accounts in organizational contexts across disciplines and industries. Leaders should also be aware of these dilemmas so they can adequately support their employees.

The approach is abductive in nature in that categorization and theory gradually develop through the exploration of insights that arise in dialogue with practitioners who work with and within the phenomena described by the theory (Peirce, 1903). Input comes both from student memos and from discussions of memos during teaching sessions. The study is an attempt to engage a phenomenon from the perspective of those living it (Corley, 2015). A methodological assumption borrowed from grounded theory is that the executive students who contributed to this study are knowledgeable agents who know what they are trying to do and can explain their thoughts, intentions and actions (Gioia, Corley, & Hamilton, 2013). The study is an effort to make sense of a complex reality, starting with an invitation to practitioners to share their experiences with ethical dilemmas in their work with social media. The analytical process consisted of (1) interpreting written input from the executive students, (2) discussing their examples with them in the classroom, (3) returning to the informants with suggested categories and (4) rewriting and modifying the categories.

Martela (2015) claimed that the novel theoretical insights that arise from abductive inquiry should be judged according to the practical usability of the proposed views for the particular actors working with and within the phenomena described in the theory. A similar assumption guides the current study, which aims to generate a theory to support and enhance ethically responsible decision-making and behavior in the use of social media by practitioners whose organizational roles resemble those of the students who contributed to the study.

Data collection for this book occurred in a teaching context, so the findings are also relevant for teaching purposes, particularly those aimed at preparing practitioners for ethical challenges at work. With a model for categorizing ethical dilemmas in place, individuals, groups and organizations can prepare for encounters with such dilemmas in their use of social media. Ethical training can be effective in generating responsible decision-making and behavior (Kaptein, 2015; Valentine & Fleischman, 2004). A set of example dilemmas and categories can help to structure the training. Weber (2007) identified inductive learning as a particularly satisfying and productive approach to teaching ethics because it encourages the learner to reflect on concrete examples. This book aims to create a foundation for such learning.

The book is organized as follows: The next chapter presents and discusses the dilemma categories that emerged from the student memos. This is followed by a chapter that presents the Navigation Wheel as a tool for analyzing about ethical dilemmas on social media. The final chapter outlines consequences for leadership in organizations in which social media is at the core of the digital transformation, and it supplies a final thought on how ethics on social media encompass considerations about doing good and avoiding harm.

References

Bakir, V., & McStay, A. (2018). Fake news and the economy of emotions: Problems, causes, solutions. *Digital Journalism, 6*(2), 154–175.

Bender, J. L., Cyr, A. B., Arbuckle, L., & Ferris, L. E. (2017). Ethics and privacy implications of using the internet and social media to recruit participants for health research: A privacy-by-design framework for online recruitment. *Journal of Medical Internet Research, 19*(4), e104.

Bertrand, C.-J. (2018). *Media ethics and accountability systems*. London and New York: Routledge.

Brinkmann, J. (2005). Understanding insurance customer dishonesty: Outline of a situational approach. *Journal of Business Ethics, 61*(2), 183–197.

Brown, M. E., Treviño, L. K., & Harrison, D. A. (2005). Ethical leadership: A social learning perspective for construct development and testing. *Organizational Behavior and Human Decision Processes, 97*(2), 117–134.

Corley, K. G. (2015). A commentary on "what grounded theory is …" engaging a phenomenon from the perspective of those living it. *Organizational Research Methods, 18*(4), 600–605.

Devereux, L., Melewar, T., & Foroudi, P. (2017). Corporate identity and social media: Existence and extension of the organization. *International Studies of Management & Organization, 47*(2), 110–134.

Duffy, A., & Knight, M. (2019). Don't be stupid: The role of social media policies in journalistic boundary-setting. *Journalism Studies, 20*(7), 932–951.

Egorov, M., Verdorfer, A. P., & Peus, C. (2018). Taming the emotional dog: Moral intuition and ethically-oriented leader development. *Journal of Business Ethics, 160*(3), 1–18.

Fenwick, T. (2016). Social media, professionalism and higher education: A sociomaterial consideration. *Studies in Higher Education, 41*(4), 664–677.

Gelinas, L., Pierce, R., Winkler, S., Cohen, I. G., Lynch, H. F., & Bierer, B. E. (2017). Using social media as a research recruitment tool: Ethical issues and recommendations. *The American Journal of Bioethics, 17*(3), 3–14.

Gioia, D. A., Corley, K. G., & Hamilton, A. L. (2013). Seeking qualitative rigor in inductive research: Notes on the Gioia methodology. *Organizational Research Methods, 16*(1), 15–31.

Goodpaster, K. E. (1992). Business ethics. In L. C. Becker & C. B. Becker (Eds.), *Encyclopedia of ethics*. New York: Garland Publishing.

Iggers, J. (2018). *Good news, bad news: Journalism ethics and the public interest*. New York and London: Routledge.

Kahneman, D. (2013). *Thinking, fast and slow*. New York: Farrar, Straus and Giroux.

Kane, G. C. (2017). The evolutionary implications of social media for organizational knowledge management. *Information and Organization, 27*(1), 37–46.

Kaplan, A. M., & Haenlein, M. (2010). Users of the world, unite! The challenges and opportunities of social media. *Business Horizons, 53*(1), 59–68.

Kaptein, M. (2015). The effectiveness of ethics programs: The role of scope, composition, and sequence. *Journal of Business Ethics, 132*(2), 415–431.

Kieran, M. (2002). *Media ethics*. London: Routledge.

Kosinski, M., Matz, S. C., Gosling, S. D., Popov, V., & Stillwell, D. (2015). Facebook as a research tool for the social sciences: Opportunities, challenges, ethical considerations, and practical guidelines. *American Psychologist, 70*(6), 543.

Kvalnes, Ø. (2019). *Moral reasoning at work: Rethinking ethics in organizations* (2nd ed.). London: Palgrave Macmillan.

Kvalnes, Ø., & Øverenget, E. (2012). Ethical navigation in leadership training. *Etikk i praksis-Nordic Journal of Applied Ethics, 6*(1), 58–71.

Lazer, D. M., Baum, M. A., Benkler, Y., Berinsky, A. J., Greenhill, K. M., Menczer, F., … Rothschild, D. (2018). The science of fake news. *Science, 359*(6380), 1094–1096.

Maclagan, P. (2003). Varieties of moral issue and dilemma: A framework for the analysis of case material in business ethics education. *Journal of Business Ethics, 48*(1), 21–32.

Maclagan, P. (2012). Conflicting obligations, moral dilemmas and the development of judgement through business ethics education. *Business Ethics: A European Review, 21*(2), 183–197.

Martela, F. (2015). Fallible inquiry with ethical ends-in-view: A pragmatist philosophy of science for organizational research. *Organization Studies, 36*(4), 537–563.

McKlindon, D., Jacobson, J. A., Nathanson, P., Walter, J. K., Lantos, J. D., & Feudtner, C. (2016). Ethics rounds: In the eye of a social media storm. *Pediatrics, 138*(3), e20161398.

Mittelstadt, B. D., & Floridi, L. (2016). The ethics of big data: Current and foreseeable issues in biomedical contexts. *Science and Engineering Ethics, 22*(2), 303–341.

Müller, R., Packendorff, J., & Sankaran, S. (2017). Balanced leadership: A new perspective for leadership in organizational project management. In S. Sankaran, R. Müller, & N. Drouin (Eds.), *Cambridge handbook of organizational project management*. Cambridge: Cambridge University Press.

Ott, L., & Theunissen, P. (2015). Reputations at risk: Engagement during social media crises. *Public Relations Review, 41*(1), 97–102.

Palacios-González, C. (2015). The ethics of clinical photography and social media. *Medicine, Health Care and Philosophy, 18*(1), 63–70.

Peirce, C. S. (1903). Pragmatism and the logic of abduction. In *The essential Peirce: Selected philosophical writings* (Vol. 2, pp. 226–242). Bloomington: Indiana University Press.

Pennycook, G., & Rand, D. G. (2019). Lazy, not biased: Susceptibility to partisan fake news is better explained by lack of reasoning than by motivated reasoning. *Cognition, 188*, 39–50.

Toffler, B. L. (1986). *Tough choices: Managers talk ethics*. New York: Wiley.

Valentine, S., & Fleischman, G. (2004). Ethics training and businesspersons' perceptions of organizational ethics. *Journal of Business Ethics, 52*(4), 391–400.

Ward, S. J. (2005). Philosophical foundations for global journalism ethics. *Journal of Mass Media Ethics, 20*(1), 3–21.

Warnick, B. R., Bitters, T. A., Falk, T. M., & Kim, S. H. (2016). Social media use and teacher ethics. *Educational Policy, 30*(5), 771–795.

Weber, J. A. (2007). Business ethics training: Insights from learning theory. *Journal of Business Ethics, 70*(1), 61–85.

Wells, D. M., Lehavot, K., & Isaac, M. L. (2015). Sounding off on social media: The ethics of patient storytelling in the modern era. *Academic Medicine, 90*(8), 1015–1019.

Open Access This chapter is licensed under the terms of the Creative Commons Attribution 4.0 International License (http://creativecommons.org/licenses/by/4.0/), which permits use, sharing, adaptation, distribution and reproduction in any medium or format, as long as you give appropriate credit to the original author(s) and the source, provide a link to the Creative Commons licence and indicate if changes were made.

The images or other third party material in this chapter are included in the chapter's Creative Commons licence, unless indicated otherwise in a credit line to the material. If material is not included in the chapter's Creative Commons licence and your intended use is not permitted by statutory regulation or exceeds the permitted use, you will need to obtain permission directly from the copyright holder.

2

Dilemmas in Social Media: A Categorization

Abstract This chapter presents five categories of ethical dilemmas that can arise for practitioners who are responsible for social media accounts in organizations. Executive students at a European business school have provided input to the categorization. The five categories to emerge from the material are the following: role dilemmas address how the agent in social media can have multiple roles, creating confusion about ethical responsibilities; tempo dilemmas occur because the exchanges in social media happen quickly, with a high risk of making mistakes; integrity dilemmas happen when the agent is tempted or pressured to act against personal and common values and principles; speech dilemmas are situations at the threshold of what one can reasonably and adequately post through a social medium; and competence dilemmas arise when the social media experts can exploit competence gaps in their own favor, with little risk of detection.

Keywords Social media • Role dilemmas • Speech dilemmas • Tempo dilemmas • Integrity dilemmas • Competence dilemmas

This study aims to categorize ethical dilemmas encountered by employees who run the social media accounts in their organizations. These dilemmas can occur across disciplines, industries and professions. Input comes from executive students at a European business school, who, in their professional capacities, are responsible for handling Facebook, Twitter, LinkedIn, Instagram and other social media accounts on behalf of their employers. They have handed in memos describing concrete dilemmas from their everyday work. Over a five-year period, five sets of students have shared their experiences of facing situations where they have to decide between conflicting ethical considerations.

The most striking realization from initial readings of the first set of dilemma memos was that these executive students found themselves in the middle of complex and demanding ethical challenges in their daily work. It was not difficult for them to come up with vivid examples from their own work experience. They were neither outsiders nor observers of organizational ethics in action, but rather actors who regularly faced tough decisions for which there were more or less equally good ethical reasons for opposite alternatives.

A pattern that emerged in the opening stages was that of conflicting interpretations of what it means to be an active social media user. The professionals handling the social media accounts in their organizations expressed doubt and confusion regarding their own role and those of colleagues and leaders who also used different kinds of social media. It also appeared that the executive students had encountered challenges to their moral convictions and personal values. Several of them had encountered pressure to engage in activities that created moral dissonance (Kvalnes, 2019), a discrepancy between their personal moral standards and what they were expected or ordered to do. There was also substantial documentation of ethical concerns about the threshold for speaking one's mind, when colleagues and leaders were involved in harsh exchanges about controversial political and social issues.

Five categories of ethical dilemmas emerged from the research process of (1) interpreting written input from executive students, (2) discussing their examples in the classroom, (3) returning with suggested categories to the informants and (4) rewriting and modifying the categories (Table 2.1):

Table 2.1 Categories of dilemmas

Role dilemmas	Who is the agent in social media? Professional, employee, friend, owner, politician, private individual or more than one of these at the same time?
Tempo dilemmas	What kind of information and opinions do we spread with the touch of a finger? What do we miss out on if we slow down and are more thoughtful?
Integrity dilemmas	To what extent should we downplay our own principles and values to gain or keep friends, followers and clients and get more likes?
Speech dilemmas	What kinds of opinions is it acceptable to express in social media? Where do we draw the line of free speech in the processes of expressing disagreement and defending ourselves against what we perceive to be unreasonable criticism?
Competence dilemmas	To what extent is it acceptable for professionals to exploit the gaps in social media competence in their own favor?

This chapter presents each of these dilemma categories in further detail, with examples from the student memos. It concludes with an outline of how the five categories overlap and how one particular dilemma can contain elements that connect it to several—and even to all five—categories.

1 Role Dilemmas

> Four of my colleagues have recently quit their jobs, and started working for a competing organization. Naturally, they remain in contact with former colleagues here, and have established friendships on Facebook, a platform that is an important arena for both organizations. Now I notice that my present colleagues share and like job-related content from those ex-colleagues, and thus help their company to spread information about their products. I think this is unacceptable, since they are assisting a competitor and undermining our own efforts to reach out to customers and become their preferred supplier of financial services.

Role dilemmas occur when the role of the person who is active in social media is unclear or open to different and conflicting interpretations. Are these words the expressions of a professional or a private person, a colleague or a friend, a company owner or a concerned citizen, an expert or a nonexpert, or a teacher or a dismayed employee? Dilemmas typically arise when the agent has one understanding of his or her role, whereas various others interpret the role differently, leading them to have conflicting ideas about what the appropriate response is.

A manager in a financial institution provided the above example. He was frustrated that his colleagues were more loyal to their friends and former colleagues than to their own organization. Their behavior suggested that they saw their role as friends as more important than their role as employees. The response this contributor received from his colleagues was that we live in an era for knowledge sharing. Social media like Facebook, LinkedIn and Twitter are designed to make information available to everybody. Knowledge hiding, where we try to gain advantages by guarding our own knowledge, is a thing of the past. It can be argued that sharing is good for the financial industry. Decision-makers must be alert and ready to develop new services and products based on insights that are available to everybody. The kind of knowledge sharing that this employee finds unacceptable actually triggers innovation and can be beneficial to all. This is an argument that can find support in research (Leonardi, 2017).

The student's reply to his colleagues was that even in a time of knowledge sharing, employees must show loyalty to their employer, particularly in situations where there is hard competition, and customer movement from one supplier to another can lead to deep economic problems for the one who is losing market shares. The role of being an employee should take priority over the role of being a friend and supporter.

Here is another example of a dilemma where decision-making becomes challenging due to confusion or uncertainty about the role, identity and position of the agent:

> One of my colleagues is responsible for our interactions with business clients, and is the outward face people associate with our unit, even on various social media platforms. However, this year she has been a participant on a popular reality show. For the younger generation, this is exciting, but I believe that our more conservative and established clients are skeptical. When the contact is through social media, people tend to be more

interested in her as a person, than in us as a company. Should she stay on in her role as head of business client relations?

In this case, the management may be reluctant to remove the employee from her position, since she generates public interest for the company, although they realize that the attention has nothing to do with her business role, and everything to do with her role in the reality show.

One student illustrated the blurred line between the agent as a professional and the agent as an engaged and enthusiastic private person:

> I am employed in an internet shop for sports equipment. It is a perfect job for me, since I am enthusiastic about the range of products in this field, and regularly use them in my private life. Can I like, comment, and share my recommendations on Facebook and other platforms as a private citizen, without informing about my professional connection to the shop?

The informant in this case sees himself as a person with high moral standards, who would only make recommendations based on his actual experiences and beliefs about the product. By being open in social media about his role in the shop, he feared that people would unreasonably start to doubt his sincerity.

Discussions in the classroom confirmed that the above are examples of a kind of ethically charged situation that a professional who is responsible for the handling of social media accounts can encounter. From the agent's point of view, the dilemmas can occur in advance of a particular interaction. How will the message I am about to publish be interpreted? Am I entitled to express it? Based on one interpretation of my role, I should not post the message, but based on another, I am in my full right to do so. Will the recipients of the message understand that I make this claim as a private citizen and not as an employee of this particular organization?

One kind of role dilemma occurs when employees use social media to go beyond their designated roles at work, to be of service to customers, or defend the organization against criticism. In their social media interactions, they may be perceived as representatives of the organizations, even though they are operating from their personal social media accounts:

I work for a railway company. We are eager to provide excellent customer service, and want to take care of the people who choose to travel with us. The service mentality is very important, and encouraged among the employees on the trains, and in the central office. However, we are not present in social media around the clock, so cannot provide immediate answers to social media inquiries about our services. The dilemma is that other employees—conductors, train drivers, technicians—who do not have access to the company's Facebook page respond to questions from travelers and the public from their personal Facebook pages. It is not part of their job description to do so, but they want to be of service and feel qualified to provide answers. The customers can mistakenly think that they are in dialogue with our official inquiry service. Some of these employees also defend the company against criticism that appear on Twitter and other social media, and may use arguments that are not in line with company policy. I encounter dilemmas where I have to respond to the eager activities of well-meaning colleagues, without causing offense to them. How do I outline the scope of action for such social media activities?

This social media administrator needs to tread carefully in addressing the situation with these colleagues. Their activities may also point to constructive alternative ways of organizing social media interaction in an organization. The voices of the people who work on the trains are authentic and real and may resonate better with the travelers than the voices of employees in central office. As is the case in other organizational contexts, delegating responsibility for social media activities to those who are closest to the core activities may stimulate a richer interaction with key stakeholders. Doing so also raises the risk of controversy and conflict, since the different individual voices may not be attuned to a common set of principles and ideas.

The input from the students indicates that role dilemmas can occur in the aftermath of an interaction. In hindsight, the agent may realize there can be more than one reasonable interpretation of a particular message or interaction, based on different understandings of his or her role. Then the choice can be made between remaining committed to the message and the way it was published and admitting that it was a mistake to express it in those terms. The sports enthusiast who also happens to work for a company that sells sports equipment may gradually realize that people have good reasons to doubt his honesty when he posts positive messages about products that can be bought from his employer.

Role dilemmas can also emerge in the context of negotiating the relationship between the person responsible for a social media account and that person's leaders or manager. Several of the informants point to their superiors' limited understanding of social media as a source of role dilemmas. When an employee has misbehaved on Facebook, some leaders delegate the responsibility to address the issue with the employee to the person who runs the Facebook account for the organization, rather than doing it themselves. When a train driver takes to Twitter to defend the organization, using sharper language than top management is comfortable with, it may fall to the person who runs the social media platforms to address the issue with the train driver. The social media professional may on the other hand think that it is the leader's responsibility to talk to the employee about it. Expertise in the field of social media is not a competence that renders a person qualified to tell an employee that he or she has overstepped an ethical line. Instead, that seems to be a responsibility tied to the role of being a leader. The final chapter of this book is dedicated to further discussion of social media ethics and leadership.

2 Tempo Dilemmas

Speed and timing emerged as another recurring feature in the input from the students. Several of them reflected on how participation in the high-tempo exchanges on social media can become compulsive and put colleagues and friends in a position where they search for constructive ways to intervene:

> I have an impulsive colleague who uses social media to immediately express his frustrations whenever we receive new guidelines and routines. People see him as a grumpy and angry person, who overreacts to the changes. We try to talk him out of expressing himself like this, but he has grown fond of the high tempo and immediate responses he gets in social media. What more can we, his colleagues, do?

There is also a role dimension to this situation, since it can be unclear whether the colleague in question will be interpreted as a professional or as a private or personal agent in these exchanges.

Tempo dilemmas gradually emerged as a useful and relevant category during the exchanges with informants to this study. Things happen very fast in social media, and part of the attraction is to participate in a pulsating activity where intuitions are at play. The distinction that Kahneman (2013) has drawn between fast and impulsive (System 1) decision-making and slow and analytic (System 2) decision-making is relevant in this context. In the first chapter, it was used to explain the difference between moral intuition (System 1) and ethical analysis (System 2). Here, it can serve to highlight the fact that social media are designed for fast and impulsive decisions and exchanges, rather than slow and analytic ones. People who rely on the latter, when they are on Twitter or Facebook, are likely to feel that the discussion they wanted to contribute to has moved on and that their carefully crafted and more thoughtful expressions and phrases are no longer relevant.

Input from the executive students indicates that traditional leaders find the high tempo of social media particularly challenging, making them wary of entering into conversations in the digital domain. The leaders' dilemma is that, on the one hand, they are concerned about losing control on a communication platform characterized by rapid exchanges of words, where you may regret some of the messages you impulsively post, and on the other hand, they are afraid to miss out on business opportunities by staying away.

Some dilemmas in social media can have both a role and a tempo dimension in them, as in the example with the impulsive colleague, mentioned above. People can be quick and eager to join the fast timeline on Twitter and end up ignoring their roles in the organization. Here are some examples that came up in the teaching sessions:

- A CEO who uses the organization's account to express her personal views on the upbringing of children or on political matters—issues that lie far beyond her professional competence.
- A researcher who uses his professional account to raise harsh criticism about a particular aspect of the welfare system in his country.

- An engineer who publicizes sexually charged comments from a conference he attends on behalf of the organization.
- A CFO who responds to reasonable criticism of one of the organization's products by going into a harsh and heated public dialogue with the sender.

Other people in the organization may be observers of this kind of rash behavior and can then encounter a choice between giving critical input to the agent and remaining silent. In some cases, this is a real dilemma, in that it is of high importance to stop the agent from putting himself or herself and the organization into further trouble; on the other hand, however, it may be a bad career move, since it may not be appreciated by the agent. In other cases, it is a false dilemma, as it is clearly appropriate to intervene and the personal cost of doing so is not all that high; it is, nevertheless, tempting to turn a blind eye to the situation to avoid personal trouble.

The high tempo of the exchanges on social media increases the likelihood of making mistakes. When things do go wrong, the person responsible for social media accounts faces dilemmas about how to cope with the situation. The opening example in the previous chapter can serve as an illustration of such an ex post tempo dilemma. The construction manager takes photos from a tunnel project in the mountains, and the communications person in the organization quickly posts them on Facebook. It provides a fresh, current and immediate report from the construction site, but one of the photos documents an HSE violation. Given the slower tempo in the publishing process, that mistake would most likely have been avoided in the days before social media. The decision-maker could have studied the photo more carefully before publication and might have spotted the violation—an employee not wearing a helmet. It was a social media mistake to publish and document the HSE mistake. In the aftermath of such events, the typical dilemma is to negotiate a balance between transparency and openness, on the one hand, and a concern for stakeholders like the employee, on the other.

Tempo dilemmas on social media also raise concerns over moral luck. Philosophers Nagel (1979) and Williams (1981) brought attention to how actual outcomes affect moral judgments of what people do. Research confirms that people tend to judge unlucky agents more harshly than lucky ones, even in the moral domain (Martin & Cushman, 2016). The difference tends to disappear with a more careful and reflective consideration of the agent's contribution and lack of control (Kneer & Machery, 2019). The difference between the immediate and intuitive judgments on the one hand and the slower and more analytic ones on the other follows the pattern of Kahneman's (2013) System 1 vs. System 2 line of thinking. When people spend time reflecting on the risk and the uncontrollable circumstances, they are less likely to judge the unlucky agent more harshly. That may be of little consolation to a professional who expects others to judge her impulsively and immediately, based on the actual outcomes of her behavior. Fear of bad moral luck can make employees wary of entering the high-tempo domain of social media.

A person responsible for running the social media accounts of an organization is exposed to moral luck, in the sense that actual outcomes of the high-tempo decisions he or she makes at work influence the moral judgments of those decisions, even though much of what happens is beyond that person's control. As in other areas of organizational life, people who operate in high-tempo and high-risk work environments deserve support and encouragement from superiors who understand the uncertain nature of the decision-making processes. An underlying feature of responses from the informants to this study is that they experience a lack of understanding from their leaders of the risks that naturally follow from operating in the high-tempo context of social media. It is not a viable option to drastically reduce the tempo of the decision-making to reduce the likelihood of making mistakes, since the existing tempo is essential to the function and thrill of social media.

3   Integrity Dilemmas

A third category to emerge from the material is that of integrity dilemmas. Presence on social media can put the integrity of individuals, groups and organizations under pressure, in that they can face situations where it is difficult to remain committed to their principles and values. They may experience moral dissonance (Kvalnes, 2019), a conflict between their moral convictions and what they are ordered or expected to do. One student gave the following example of how her organization found itself in a situation where doing the right thing, from the perspective of professional integrity, potentially jeopardized a commercial relation:

> We are an applied research organization, offering clients research reports about their products. One of our clients started to use a production method that some of our researchers found would put the end users at risk, if they failed to take proper precautions. Our client did not see the need to inform the public or their customers about these facts. We needed to decide whether to, nevertheless, use social media and other sources to inform about the need to take precautions. In the process, we risked becoming unpopular with the client who produced it. In the end, we used all means possible to spread information to the public, and put the relation to a big client to the test.

In this case, professional integrity trumped concerns about losing out on further assignments from the client. In its application of social media, the organization gave priority to the value of food safety over potentially negative economic outcomes. They found a way of doing so that turned out to be acceptable to the client and so did not lead to a commercial loss. We can study even this process through the lens of moral luck. It was risky to prioritize their own principles over the wishes of the client, but the actual outcome somehow justifies that decision, even if factors beyond the decision-makers' control may have influenced how things turned out.

Integrity is central to how individuals, groups and organizations preserve unity over time (Cox, La Caze, & Levine, 2018). A person or organization of integrity builds decision-making and behavior on a set of stable standards and principles. These are not open to negotiation. There can be tensions between different kinds of integrity, as between professional and personal integrity, where commitment to work-related standards can conflict with commitment to standards that are central to life outside of work. We can interpret the example above as a conflict between professional and public service-oriented integrity, on the one hand, and commercial integrity, on the other. A core component in the latter kind of integrity is to be of service to the clients and their needs.

Integrity dilemmas can occur in a range of exchanges within the framework of social media. In classroom discussions, the executive students described situations where the ambition to increase the number of friends or followers (and thus reach out to potential clients or customers) one has on social media can make it tempting to:

- Like and share content that you actually find uninteresting, uninspiring and even questionable or wrong.
- Refrain from speaking up against content that you disagree with or find appalling.

Both of these responses depend on putting your own moral convictions and beliefs aside to become and remain popular with actual or potential friends and followers. To see growth in the number of followers or friends on social media, management in an organization may expect their employees to keep personal convictions and values in check, even when these are well-aligned with what the organization itself is supposed to stand for. It can be a matter of sacrificing both personal integrity and organizational integrity to become and remain popular in the eyes of potential clients.

Personal ambitions to remain popular and well-liked can also make it tempting to compromise individual values:

> My organization promotes contemporary music, and we struggle to reach out to audiences in an effective manner. We are active on Facebook, and share information and sell tickets to events. From the music community, we are under constant pressure to share and like their events, both as an organization and individually. On my private Facebook and Twitter accounts I can choose which events to recommend, like, and share. Can I single out content that I think is good and worth spreading, and be more selective in what I help to promote? That is what I want to do, since it hurts to recommend trash. If I follow my values, I will become unpopular in many quarters, where my name and profile is well known.

It hurts to recommend trash, even if it may have other positive consequences. This decision-maker frequently faces situations where it can be profitable to downplay personal and organizational values for the sake of popularity. However, the gains may only be temporary and short term. Research on corporate identity and values indicates that keeping one's organizational integrity intact is good for long-term profitability. Commitment to a stable set of values can be instrumental to corporate flourishing (Chye Koh & Boo, 2004; Collins & Porras, 1996) and make employees less likely to leave the organization (Haque, Fernando, & Caputi, 2019). Sacrificing organizational and professional integrity for popularity on social media is risky, but it can be what organizations expect from those who run their social media outlets.

Some dilemmas have a role dimension, as well as an integrity dimension to them. One student shared an example from her job as part of the editorial team of a lifestyle magazine. The owners of the magazine had recently decided to hire an advertising bureau to run their Twitter and Instagram accounts, to make the use of those platforms more professional. People from the bureau posed as journalists from the magazine and invited people to meet "us" at different destinations. The actual journalists were unhappy about this arrangement and argued that the users would be conned into thinking that they were actually meeting real representatives from the magazine. The owners created role confusion, and the journalists faced a test of their integrity. They had to decide whether they were willing to work for a magazine that hired externals to run their social media platforms in this manner.

The majority of executive students who reflected on this dilemma in the auditorium tended to sympathize with the journalists and agreed that it was an affront to their personal and professional integrity to accept that externals would run their social media accounts. However, when the author presented the same dilemma to a younger group of students (20–25 years of age), a different response pattern emerged. These students tended to find it unproblematic to hire a bureau to run the social media accounts for an organization and even claim to have readers meet "us" at events.

Integrity dilemmas occur on personal, group and organizational levels. Their common feature is that the decision-maker's values and principles are tested. Several of the informants to this study describe how their roles of running social media accounts on behalf of their organizations regularly put them in the middle of situations where they can defend and protect integrity on all three levels, or sacrifice it for economic or other gain. It thus seems important to prepare professionals who are assigned to such roles for these kinds of dilemmas.

4 Speech Dilemmas

What kinds of standpoints and views are acceptable to express on social media? This is the question behind a range of examples provided by the informants to this study. They have faced situations where one set of considerations supports the publication of an expression and another set of considerations goes against it. Speech dilemma was a category name proposed, tested and accepted for this kind of situation early in the study. A typical situation is that the organization receives harsh criticism on social media, based on a misrepresentation of facts:

> I work in a bank in my hometown. After having financed the startup of a local company, we decided to say no to further loans to finance expansion plans. The company went bankrupt some months later, since it was not able to collect capital from other sources. The owner felt that our "no" came at a time where the company was about to turn a corner, while our decision was based on an evaluation of past events, communication, risk, market development, and so on. When the bankruptcy occurred, the owner used Facebook to attack the bank and employees and managers within it, hitting us with false information about the process. How were we supposed to respond? We could, of course, not use factual and sensitive information, and correct his version. One possibility was to give a general reply that our decisions are always based on an evaluation of the totality, and that our clients sometimes would disagree about interpretation of the facts, and so remind people that there are always at least two sides to a case. We decided to do nothing, and now see this experience as an example of how powerful Facebook can be, and how powerless you can be in responding to criticism expressed there.

In this situation, the bank apparently found itself in a false dilemma, since the alternative of using Facebook to actively respond to the false allegations was ethically and legally wrong. There was a scope of action for a more general response, which did not include the revelation of sensitive information, but the bank decided against it, since that response probably would have prolonged the time it spent in the public spotlight.

Other examples in the data follow a similar pattern to the one above. In one, a restaurant faces the choice between defending itself against false social media accusations from a bad-tempered customer and remaining calm. The problem with the latter response is that the digital traces of the criticism are likely to remain, turning up when potential customers search for information before they determine whether to come there for a meal. A nonresponse can be interpreted as acceptance of the allegations.

With traditional publication channels, it is up to the editors to decide what to publish. With social media, this decision level has disappeared, and the agents who consider the publication of personal messages and messages on behalf of organizations must account for ethical aspects. The absence of the traditional editorial processes prior to publishing means that questionable messages can be posted, reaching a wide audience. People can inflict pain on themselves and others, as in the following example:

> A colleague is sharing very personal and sensitive information about her own mental health and how it affects her family life. I believe it worsens the situation for the children in the family. Her own view is that problems should be shared, and that openness is a good thing. Her texts are sometimes posted openly on Facebook, and sometimes within a group of Facebook friends. Some of her claims are also about conditions at work, and her frustrations with our organization. "This job is killing me" and "I don't have the energy to turn up at the office today" are examples of what she posts on Facebook.

Colleagues of this person face the task of finding adequate ways to respond. The situation is similar to one of the tempo dilemmas discussed earlier, the difference being that here, the questionable openness is not caused by impulsiveness and the high tempo of the medium; rather, it flows from a sense of freedom to express whatever one wants, without interference from anybody.

Social media provide platforms for free speech and political activism (McCarthy, 2017; Shirky, 2011). They have also become platforms for trolling, hate speech, harassment, fake news and other kinds of misinformation (Bakir & McStay, 2018; Craker & March, 2016; Hannan, 2018; Lazer et al., 2018; Nicol, 2012; Pennycook & Rand, 2019). Providers like Facebook and Twitter are expected to function as moderators, to maintain some ethical standards concerning the flow of information they allow. The general ethical tension is between promoting free speech, on the one hand, and being on guard against harmful expressions, on the other. Political exchanges on social media can sometimes include rude and hateful expressions. The importance of moderating the exchanges is underlined by research, documenting the contagiousness of trolling and harassment on social media. People who are normally well behaved tend to adopt harassing behavior if they are regularly exposed to that kind of behavior (Cheng, Danescu-Niculescu-Mizil, Leskovec, & Bernstein, 2017). The handling of speech dilemmas and questions of what to publish can therefore have practical consequences.

Some speech dilemmas are also closely linked to role dilemmas, as when researchers get personally involved in political debate on matters they have knowledge about through their work:

> I work with researchers who provide important input to political processes on a national level. Some of them participate in discussions on social media about issues related to their expertise. In a range of cases, their personal political views shine through. We are concerned about the researchers' freedom of speech, but when their political preferences become evident in public, it can negatively affect the trust in their independence and objectivity as researchers. We are planning to formulate guidelines for their activities in social media.

An initiative to establish guidelines or a code of conduct can be commendable, because it raises up to a principled level the issue of when and how it is acceptable for researchers and other practitioners to express their personal views on social media (Lipschultz, 2017). However, attempts to demarcate between acceptable and unacceptable expressions can be seen as an infringement on the researchers' autonomy. Detailed guidelines may also inadvertently lead to loophole ethics or the attitude that anything they are silent about is acceptable (Kvalnes, 2019).

When employees explore the limits of their freedom to express their views through social media, it may fall to their colleagues, rather than their leader, to address the issue with them. The following situation is representative of what the executive student informants in this study claim to face when a colleague behaves in a manner that the management finds unacceptable:

> I am working for a public directorate. The minster has initiated dramatic changes in our procedures. One of my colleagues is very critical of these changes, based on his expertise and experience. He uses Twitter to express his criticism of the minister's initiative, and receives so much attention that even the non-digital management in the directorate gets to hear about it. Now they ask me, as a representative of the communications unit, to tell the colleague to stop using Twitter to express his critical views. How should I proceed?

Here, we have a situation where the management steps away from a testing set of circumstances and leaves the responsibility of taking action with the person who has the most social media competence. As such, it takes the form of a role dilemma, where the agent must decide whether to follow orders to do a manager's job. It seems that it is actually the management's responsibility to address the issue with the employee causing alarm with his social media use, but the task is instead pushed to the person most competent in the use of the technology. That person can also face an integrity dilemma, in that he or she may feel that following orders, in this case, requires a sacrifice of personal values and principles.

In this section, we have seen that a range of dilemmas on social media are connected to speech and expression, and where to draw the line regarding content that can hurt the sender or receiver of messages posted on social media. The examples show that speech dilemmas tend to overlap with dilemmas in the other categories. Depending on perspective, a dilemma situation may be described in terms of role, tempo, integrity and speech. This tendency to overlap is addressed toward the end of the chapter.

5 Competence Dilemmas

The first and second rounds of memos and discussions with the informants in this study gave rise to four tentative categories of dilemmas. Students and researchers were able to agree that the examples fit into the categories of role dilemmas, tempo dilemmas, integrity dilemmas and speech dilemmas. However, another set of examples did not fit properly into any of these categories. Experienced users of social media explained how they had built up professionalism and competence, and tended to meet internal stakeholders (leaders/managers, colleagues) and external stakeholders (customers, clients, competitors, authorities) who, by contrast, were novices. They raised the following ethical question: To what extent is it acceptable to exploit the competence gap to one's own benefit?

Internally, a competence dilemma can occur when social media experts interact with colleagues and leaders who have limited experience with the workings of those communication channels. It puts the experts in a powerful position. The competence gap makes it possible for them to influence internal processes in ways that are invisible to others. Both of the candidates for an internal promotion may need some guidance in social media usage, to increase their chances of getting the job. The social media expert can observe that this is the case and decide whether to offer guidance. Informants to this study have described how withholding or offering social media support can be an effective way of influencing the progress of a colleague's career or the direction of a particular internal project.

Competence dilemmas also arise in the context of external relations. One informant described a situation where she was able to get a profitable assignment for her organization by introducing clients to social media platforms that they may have lacked the competence to master:

> We have clients in professions that do not have a tradition for written communication, like industry workers, craftsmen, and health care personnel. They can potentially make good use of Facebook to reach the strategic goals with their small companies, but sense that they do not master the language well enough to use it. They are afraid of being arrested by the "language police" for misspellings and grammatical mistakes. Many of

their clients are well educated, and more fluent in the written language, and if they experience lack of language mastery from the supplier, it may reduce the trust level. What should we advise our clients to do?

The best advice to these "illiterate" clients may be to find other platforms for communicating with the outside world. From the consultant's own perspective, however, it is more profitable to secure an assignment in which she can guide the clients into the social media world. A third option may be to be open about the risks of exposing one's lack of language mastery and honest about the efforts it will take to, nevertheless, make good use of Facebook, Twitter or other social media platforms. That option puts the clients in a position to make an informed decision about the way forward.

The category of competence dilemmas can account for situations that follow the pattern of the situation described above. They occur in provider–client relationships, where the provider can exploit a competence gap in relation to the client. This can be done by (1) offering social media services that the client has little or no use for and (2) pricing the services higher than their actual market value. The professional may be an expert on social media use and sell services that the client lacks the competence to evaluate, and the imbalance introduces the possible misuse of client trust. On this description, competence dilemmas belong under the heading of false dilemmas. They are examples of conflict-of-interest situations, where it is ethically appropriate to prioritize client interest over self-interest, but economically tempting to do otherwise, particularly since the client lacks competence to realize that it is happening. As such, they are at the core of professional ethics (Nanda, 2003).

The informants to this study have been invited to share dilemmas connected to their roles as being responsible for social media accounts in the organizations. In these initial roles, they are not engaged in a provider–client relationship, and so the issue of competence dilemmas seems to be irrelevant. However, many of the informants have experience in taking on the additional role of advising clients about social media use, based on their competence in that area. As such, there are situations that professionals who assume such positions and roles should prepare for.

Some informants have been skeptical of the competence dilemma category, because they can envisage situations where exploiting a competence gap in their own favor is perfectly natural. This is what normally occurs in a competitive business environment, both within a company and in relation to external competitors. If others are less competent, then that provides a reason to move forward and take advantage, rather than back off for ethical reasons. This misgiving points to a need to be precise in the description of the category. A competence dilemma in relation to external actors does not occur in connection with any kind of competence gap. It typically arises when there are clients or customers who assume that the professional will give priority to their interest, rather than self-interest. The social media expert is in a position to prioritize self-interest without detection. These conflict-of-interest situations serve to test the professional's willingness to do the right thing (serve the client) and not give in to the temptation of giving priority to self-interest. As such, they are structurally similar to conflict-of-interest situations that can occur in any professional setting where a competence gap is present.

6   A Spectrum of Dilemmas

A discovery that emerged in the analysis of the student data was that one particular dilemma can include aspects from more than one of the categories outlined here and may, to some extent, belong in all five categories. The examples are not necessarily deep or complex. The following situation is one where the dimensions of role, tempo, integrity, speech and competence all are present:

> One of my clients wants to give a finder's fee to people who would tip her about potential employees for a particular project. She wants me to help her share and spread the information in social media, through our Facebook, Twitter, and LinkedIn accounts. However, we also have clients who are in competition with her company, so am reluctant to do so. If I decline, it will hurt our relation to the client, but the alternative will most likely provoke other clients. What should I do?

The agent here is in a dual role, as the supplier of one particular client who expects help, but also as a supplier for other clients. The situation demands a quick response and is one where there is little opportunity for slow and careful deliberation. It puts the supplier's integrity to the test, as there appears to be a conflict between what he or she thinks is the right thing to do (decline the request) and what it is tempting to do (honor the request). The speech dimension is also present, in that the agent must consider what it is acceptable for him or her to say, while the agent's competence in the use of social media is also in play.

Another example can further illustrate how several dilemma categories can be relevant to one situation:

> Both Amnesty International and Greenpeace have international campaigns against my organization, with special emphasis on operations outside our own country. I think the campaigns are spreading misinformation about my employer, and personally wish to correct them. However, I work in the communications unit in my organization, and anything I express in social media can be interpreted as the organization's response to the allegations in the campaigns.

This agent faces a role dilemma, in that any personal expressions can be interpreted as being made on behalf of the organization. The high tempo of the exchanges on social media leaves an opening for impulsive responses that may not be beneficial for the agent or the organization. Integrity is at stake, in that the agent may have strong convictions that favor speaking up to confront misinformation and, at the same time, realize that there is a professional cost to doing so. Personal integrity may thus dictate a different approach to that favored by professional integrity. There is clearly a speech dimension to the dilemma, in that there are ethical costs attached to speaking up as well as to remaining silent. A competence aspect is that the agent is a knowledgeable person when it comes to the workings of social media, and therefore knows how the assumed misinformation can spread and become accepted as reliable and factual, and is also familiar with ways to counter that development.

It is not surprising that ethical dilemmas in the sphere of social media use in organizations can have aspects that fit with more than one and even with all five of the dilemma categories outlined in this chapter. The realities under scrutiny are multifaceted and can have overlapping features that are all ethically relevant.

A theoretical implication is that the proposed concepts and characterizations of dilemmas must reflect their ambiguity and richness. Instead of presenting the five categories as a list, it can be even more useful to place them in a model that acknowledges the possibility of more than one adequate description.

The question to ask, regarding one particular dilemma, may be to what extent it belongs under one categorization or under more than one. A dilemma may primarily be a role dilemma but also have some features that make it into an integrity dilemma or a tempo dilemma. Another dilemma may, most strikingly, be a speech dilemma but, in addition, belong under the heading of a competence dilemma. The model can also serve as a tool to express disagreement about the ethical core of a particular dilemma and thereby bring misunderstanding to the surface. People who apparently disagree about a course of action in a dilemma may actually do so because they have adopted different interpretations and categorizations of the situation at hand. It is well known that the framing of dilemmas can affect decision-making and choices (Cubitt, Drouvelis, & Gächter, 2011; Fleishman, 1988; Fosgaard, Hansen, & Wengström, 2019), and the current model can help bring framing differences to the surface.

The category model articulated above can serve as a starting point for moral reasoning about activities in social media and may turn out to need further elaboration. There may be ethical challenges for organizational users of social media that the framework does not capture adequately. Each of the five categories may have a potential for subcategories, to make the conceptualization more fine-tuned to the practitioners' experienced realities. For now, the model can serve as a tentative tool to zoom in on questions about ethically right and wrong, permissible, obligatory and forbidden actions in the use of social media in organizational settings, to assist practitioners in becoming aware of and handling ethical dilemmas at work.

It should also be clear that the overall categorization is not unique to social media. Clearly, there can be role dilemmas, tempo dilemmas, integrity dilemmas, speech dilemmas and competence dilemmas in organizational contexts that are unrelated to social media. The ambition here has not been to come up with dilemma categories that are present solely in relation to social media use in organizations. The descriptions in Fig. 2.1 connect the category labels more specifically to social media, but the general labels can be applied more widely in organizations.

This chapter has presented five categories of ethical dilemmas for professionals who run the social media accounts for organizations. The categorization builds on input from executive students at a European business school, all of whom work on digital transformation processes in their organizations and, more specifically, have a hand in running the social media platforms for the employers. The five categories, consisting of role dilemmas, tempo dilemmas, integrity dilemmas, speech dilemmas and competence dilemmas, emerged from a close reading of input from around 250 students. One and the same dilemma may have elements that place it in more than one of the categories. For practitioners, the categorization can assist them in reflecting systematically on the kinds of situations they may encounter at work. The next chapter proposes cognitive tools for going a step further, enabling the practitioners to analyze

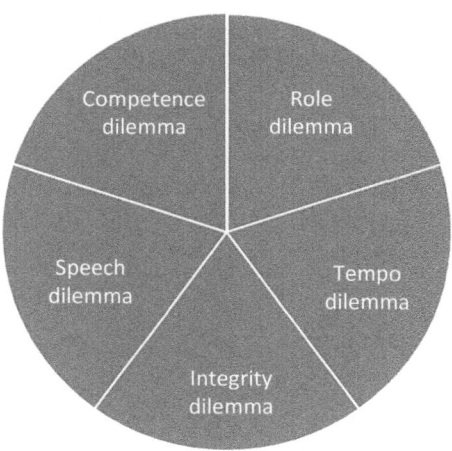

Fig. 2.1 Spectrum of dilemmas

the dilemma at hand and reach a conclusion regarding the appropriate course of action.

References

Bakir, V., & McStay, A. (2018). Fake news and the economy of emotions: Problems, causes, solutions. *Digital Journalism, 6*(2), 154–175.
Cheng, J., Danescu-Niculescu-Mizil, C., Leskovec, J., & Bernstein, M. (2017). Anyone can become a troll. *American Scientist, 105*(3), 152.
Chye Koh, H., & Boo, E. F. H. (2004). Organisational ethics and employee satisfaction and commitment. *Management Decision, 42*(5), 677–693.
Collins, J. C., & Porras, J. I. (1996). Building your company's vision. *Harvard Business Review, 74*(5), 65.
Cox, D., La Caze, M., & Levine, M. P. (2018). *Integrity and the fragile self.* London: Routledge.
Craker, N., & March, E. (2016). The dark side of Facebook®: The dark tetrad, negative social potency, and trolling behaviours. *Personality and Individual Differences, 102*, 79–84.
Cubitt, R. P., Drouvelis, M., & Gächter, S. (2011). Framing and free riding: Emotional responses and punishment in social dilemma games. *Experimental Economics, 14*(2), 254–272.
Fleishman, J. A. (1988). The effects of decision framing and others' behavior on cooperation in a social dilemma. *Journal of Conflict Resolution, 32*(1), 162–180.
Fosgaard, T. R., Hansen, L. G., & Wengström, E. (2019). Cooperation, framing, and political attitudes. *Journal of Economic Behavior & Organization, 158*, 416–427.
Hannan, J. (2018). Trolling ourselves to death? Social media and post-truth politics. *European Journal of Communication, 33*(2), 214–226.
Haque, A., Fernando, M., & Caputi, P. (2019). The relationship between responsible leadership and organisational commitment and the mediating effect of employee turnover intentions: An empirical study with Australian employees. *Journal of Business Ethics, 156*(3), 759–774.
Kahneman, D. (2013). *Thinking, fast and slow.* New York: Farrar, Straus and Giroux.
Kneer, M., & Machery, E. (2019). No luck for moral luck. *Cognition, 182*, 331–348.

Kvalnes, Ø. (2019). *Moral reasoning at work: Rethinking ethics in organizations* (2nd ed.). London: Palgrave Macmillan.

Lazer, D. M., Baum, M. A., Benkler, Y., Berinsky, A. J., Greenhill, K. M., Menczer, F., ... Rothschild, D. (2018). The science of fake news. *Science, 359*(6380), 1094–1096.

Leonardi, P. M. (2017). The social media revolution: Sharing and learning in the age of leaky knowledge. *Information and Organization, 27*(1), 47–59.

Lipschultz, J. H. (2017). *Social media communication: Concepts, practices, data, law and ethics.* New York: Routledge.

Martin, J. W., & Cushman, F. (2016). The adaptive logic of moral luck. In *The Blackwell companion to experimental philosophy.* Hoboken, NJ: Wiley-Blackwell.

McCarthy, C. (2017). Balance social media concerns with free speech rights. *College Athletics and the Law, 14*(5), 1–5.

Nagel, T. (1979). Moral luck. In *Mortal questions*. Cambridge: Cambridge University Press.

Nanda, A. (2003). *The essence of professionalism: Managing conflict of interest: Division of research.* Harvard Business School Background Note 903–120.

Nicol, S. (2012). Cyber-bullying and trolling. *Youth Studies Australia, 31*(4), 3.

Pennycook, G., & Rand, D. G. (2019). Lazy, not biased: Susceptibility to partisan fake news is better explained by lack of reasoning than by motivated reasoning. *Cognition, 188,* 39–50.

Shirky, C. (2011). The political power of social media: Technology, the public sphere, and political change. *Foreign Affairs, 90*(1), 28–41.

Williams, B. (1981). *Moral luck: Philosophical papers 1973–1980.* Cambridge: Cambridge University Press.

Open Access This chapter is licensed under the terms of the Creative Commons Attribution 4.0 International License (http://creativecommons.org/licenses/by/4.0/), which permits use, sharing, adaptation, distribution and reproduction in any medium or format, as long as you give appropriate credit to the original author(s) and the source, provide a link to the Creative Commons licence and indicate if changes were made.

The images or other third party material in this chapter are included in the chapter's Creative Commons licence, unless indicated otherwise in a credit line to the material. If material is not included in the chapter's Creative Commons licence and your intended use is not permitted by statutory regulation or exceeds the permitted use, you will need to obtain permission directly from the copyright holder.

3

Ethical Navigation on Social Media

Abstract This chapter provides conceptual tools for systematic decision-making for agents who are facing ethical dilemmas on social media. The Navigation Wheel offers a framework for analyzing concrete ethical dilemmas. The chapter illustrates how it can be used by analyzing a speech dilemma encountered by a professional handling an organization's Facebook page. A decision-maker can take each available option through the six questions in the Wheel before moving on to make a decision—Law: Is it legal? Identity: Is it in accordance with our values? Morality: Is it right? Reputation: Does it affect our goodwill? Economy: Is it in accordance with our business objectives? Ethics: Can it be justified? Under the ethics heading, the decision-maker can apply the principle of equality and the principle of publicity to identify the ethically optional alternative. The same set of questions can also serve as a framework for ethical debriefing.

Keywords Ethical analysis • Decision-making • Social media • Ethical debriefing • Ethical dilemma

The purpose of this chapter is to propose a set of conceptual tools to analyze ethical dilemmas on social media. The same tools were applied in the teaching sessions with the executive students who contributed to this study with their memos on digital dilemmas. Practitioners can apply these tools to their everyday challenges in coping with situations in which they must prioritize between conflicting moral and other considerations. Teachers and facilitators who design ethical training for decision-makers in organizations can use them as a starting point for systematic reflection on dilemmas. The theoretical contribution is to build on existing ethical theory and make it applicable to the particular professional need to deal adequately with social media dilemmas.

The first chapter introduced a distinction between moral intuition and ethical analysis as the fast and slow modes of decision-making when facing a dilemma. The distinction is parallel to the one Kahneman (2013) drew between fast System 1 and slow System 2 decision-making. The professionals who are responsible for handling social media accounts in their organizations can decide on a course of action based on moral intuition and gut feeling about what is right or wrong in the circumstances or engage in ethical reasoning. To proceed with the latter, they need a set of principles and concepts to guide the process. The current chapter sets out to provide a framework for slow thinking about dilemmas on social media. It builds on a method developed by Kvalnes and Øverenget (2012) and elaborated by Kvalnes (2019). A central component is the Navigation Wheel, a tool that brings attention to the dimensions of law, identity, morality, reputation, economy and ethics as relevant to decision-making.

The first section of this chapter presents a situation in which a person responsible for an organization's Facebook account encounters a dilemma. The example belongs to the same data set from which the categorization in the previous chapter emerged. The chapter will proceed with two sections presenting ethical concepts and principles in an analysis of that dilemma to illustrate how they are applicable to such cases. The second and third sections present two ethical principles that decision-makers can turn to in their analysis of available options, while the fourth section demonstrates how the Navigation Wheel can guide reasoning and decision-making when facing a dilemma in the context of organizational social media use. The final section proposes a method for ethical debriefing, a process in which the decision-makers step back from the situation they have been through, take stock of the events and articulate the experience. The Navigation Wheel can serve as a cognitive tool for this kind of retrospective reflection, in which the aim is to learn from the experience of having faced an ethically challenging situation.

1 A Speech Dilemma

The memos from the executive students who provided material for this study vary in detail and richness. Some gave very brief descriptions of their dilemmas, while others gave more detailed accounts. This chapter will focus on one of the dilemmas described most vividly to exemplify a method for ethical analysis. Here is the full description of a situation briefly outlined in the opening of Chap. 1:

> One of our big construction projects is to build a long road tunnel in the mountains. It has its own Facebook page. One of my colleagues, a communications advisor, runs this page. She replies to questions and posts pictures and updates on the developments in the project. Many users follow the process and are regular visitors to the page. They like and comment on the posts. The activity generates positive energy toward the project. Sharing information on Facebook about progress and milestones creates pride among the employees. Interested locals can follow and comment on the development.

From this initial description, it is clear that this is an example of a social medium used in a positive manner. News from the construction project reaches many stakeholders and parties who take an interest in it; Facebook opens up flexible and dynamic interaction. The posts are fresh and current. Those who follow the progress of the project, both from within and outside it, can stay tuned by following and responding to the posts. Here we seem to have social media at its energizing best.

The collaboration between the communications advisor who runs the Facebook account and the main contributor to the project—the construction manager—also appears to be in good flow:

> My colleague receives photos from the project, particularly from the construction manager, who is a very good photographer. A routine has emerged where his photos are published immediately, without editing or further processing.

Based on the discussion in the previous chapter, this is where doubt can set in regarding the established collaborative routines between the communications advisor and the construction manager. The exchanges between them are very fast, with seamless steps from taking a photo and sending it to the Facebook administrator to getting it published to a wide audience. The high tempo can be exhilarating, but it also creates risk of small- and large-scale mistakes.

As the situation proceeds, it does indeed lead to publication of content that should never have been posted:

> One Thursday afternoon, my colleague receives some photos from this construction manager, which she quickly posts on Facebook before going home from work.
>
> On Friday evening, she gets a desperate phone call from the construction manager, who explains that one of the photos he has taken and that has been posted on Facebook depicts an HSE violation. The photo is from the tunnel opening, and one of the workers is not wearing a helmet.

Working without a helmet in a construction site is a major HSE violation, and now it has been documented in a Facebook post run by the organization itself. The student proceeds to explain the seriousness of the matter:

> In our organization, we have recently had a range of serious accidents because of HSE violations. In the last two years, four workers have died due to sloppy HSE work on our projects. We have gone public saying that things have changed, and that we are now prioritizing safety on all our

construction projects. It is our responsibility to monitor the subcontractors, and to make sure they abide by the HSE regulations.

The construction manager has now visited the Facebook page and seen his own photo with new eyes. The worker is clearly not wearing a helmet. More than a thousand users have seen it and some of them have posted angry messages about it. They are questioning the HSE aspect and whether we have learned anything from previous accidents and injuries.

In this unfortunate situation, a photo documenting an HSE violation has been posted and already commented upon. From the organization's point of view, it is a serious matter that (1) an HSE violation has occurred and (2) a photo of it has gone public and been spotted by concerned and critical users.

What should the communications advisor do next? The message from the person who took the photo and initially made it available for publication is clear:

> Now the construction manager calls my colleague and asks her to immediately delete the post with the photo in it to avoid further exposure of the HSE mistake. My colleague hesitates but decides to do what the construction manager asks of her.

Facebook content is removed without much reflection on alternatives and consequences. Decision-making in this situation appears to have been completely System 1 driven. The intuition of the construction manager and the Facebook administrator is to remove the content as quickly as possible before more people become aware of it and more damage is done. That intuition may not be an example of moral intuition, or a sense of what one should do under such circumstances from a moral point of view, but rather a gut feeling about how to get out of an uncomfortable situation quickly.

The decision to delete the post containing the compromising photo immediately may or may not be the most adequate response. Would the decision have been the same if the two collaborators had spent 15 minutes or more going through the available options and reasoning calmly about their merits? That is hard to tell, but reflections on what might have been done differently can at least serve to prepare the decision-makers for similar episodes later.

In the aftermath of the dramatic end to the previous week, colleagues sat down to reflect on how well the situation was handled:

> On Monday morning, the colleague comes to work and explains what she did on Friday evening. We discuss whether she did the right thing. Should she have replied to the criticism before deleting the photo? Should we now post a text about the deletion, explain the circumstances and admit the HSE mistake? What should we do if a journalist contacts us with critical questions about the HSE violation and our decision to delete without commenting?

The student memo goes on to describe that they collectively decided to do nothing more regarding the deleted post. They anxiously waited for responses from the people who had initially posted critical comments, but nothing came. Apparently, the posting mistake and the subsequent deletion of the post without addressing the users' concerns did not lead to further trouble. However, the episode had been noted by some concerned users. It is possible that some of them took a screenshot of the content and stored it for later use. Even if they have not taken action yet, they may do so later in future exchanges about HSE issues in the organization.

It is unclear from the memo whether the group who debriefed about the incident on Monday agreed that the communications advisor had dealt with it in an exemplary manner and whether she or other employees should do the same again under similar circumstances. One thing they seem to have agreed upon is to ensure better quality control ahead of publishing photos.

The following sections will suggest how ethical analysis can shed light on the situation described here to illustrate more generally how decision-makers can clarify the issues at hand before making a decision. The focus will be on the one moment in the story when the communications advisor faces a dilemma. She could either (1) respond to the users' criticism before deleting the photo or (2) delete the photo without responding to the criticism. Her quick and intuitive decision in the heat of the moment was to go for (2). Ethical analysis will either confirm that she actually did the right thing or disconfirm and suggest that (1) would have been a more responsible way to proceed. A third outcome of analysis may be that there are one or more other options that she did not consider that would have been ethically better. In general, ethical analysis can either strengthen or weaken the assumption that a choice based on initial impulse is in fact the one that ethical analysis singles out as the preferred one.

In light of the categorization in the previous chapter, the communications advisor faced a speech dilemma, as it involved a decision regarding what one should or should not express on a social medium. Prior to the situation, she seems to have encountered tempo dilemmas, in which a pattern of quick, impulsive and energizing behavior set the stage for mistakes. A slower tempo would have reduced the risk of mistakes but also reduced the excitement and thrill of using Facebook at work.

2 Principle of Equality

Consistency is a central requirement in ethical analysis and moral reasoning. It is at the core of duty ethics and Kant's categorical imperative (Kant, 1998 (1785)) but also more generally accepted across ethical theories and moral outlooks. One expression of a consistency requirement is the Golden Rule, a principle found in many religions and cultures (Wattles, 1996). It states that one should treat others in the way that one wants to be treated. The rule encourages decision-makers to imagine a turning of the tables. What if you were in that other person's shoes and they were in yours? Would you accept that the person acted toward you in the way that you are now planning to act toward that person?

Kant's consistency requirement is that the agent should act in such a way that the rule for that action could be universalized (Kant, 1983, 1998 (1785)). The agent should consider whether the actions under consideration could serve as a norm for how any other person facing the same kind of situation should act. Kant considered his categorical imperative to be an advancement of the Golden Rule because of its universal and formal nature. A limitation to the Golden Rule is that it primarily works for situations in which it is imaginable to swap places with the people who are affected by one's actions to consider what it would be like to be one of them. In many circumstances, that thought experiment is hard to conduct and limits the scope for reflection. A more universal and demanding consistency requirement emerges when we consider whether actions can serve as exemplary for all agents facing similar circumstances.

In a practical and organizational context, we can express the consistency requirement in a *principle of equality* (Kvalnes, 2019):

> Equal cases should be treated equally. A difference in treatment requires that there is a morally relevant difference between the two cases.

With this principle in hand, we can explore the precise nature of the difference between superficially similar behaviors, such as giving and receiving gifts on the one hand and giving and receiving bribes on the other. From an ethical perspective, gifts are acceptable and bribes are not. The principle of equality requires that we establish a demarcation line between the two phenomena. What do we need to know to decide whether an exchange that takes place in front of our eyes is an innocent and pure gift-giving ceremony or a dubious attempt to influence a decision-maker with a bribe? A more detailed description of the context for the exchange and the involved parties reveals whether it is the one or the other. The participants' roles and motivation are relevant, and so is the value of the item changing hands.

The principle of equality also connects to fairness at work. Employees expect fair treatment and proper justification when a colleague receives special treatment in a positive or negative manner. A leader who hands out benefits or punishments to certain employees and not to others can expect to be pressured to provide justification in terms of the morally relevant differences between those who receive and those who don't.

The communications advisor who considers how to deal with a Facebook post with a photo of an HSE violation can also think in terms of consistency. From an ethical perspective, she should attempt to find an exemplary solution that can serve as a norm for how to cope with such situations. More specifically, she can explore her options through the lens of the principle of equality. That reflection can start from an assumption that a Facebook administrator, as a rule, should reply to comments from users and not delete posts to avoid confrontation or unpleasantness. Then again, there can be exceptions to that rule. The principle requires her to identify morally relevant differences between normal situations in which she would respond to comments and not delete posts and the current one.

The principle of equality cuts across the two main traditions of normative ethics. Both duty ethics and utilitarian ethics can accept the principle but differ on what counts as a morally relevant difference. Thus, they would provide conflicting guidance to the communications advisor in her attempt to identify morally relevant aspects of the situation. In outline, the difference between the two traditions is that duty ethics prioritizes behavior and conduct (the right) over outcomes (the good), while utilitarian ethics does the opposite by prioritizing outcomes (the good) over behavior and conduct (the right) (Kvalnes, 2019). From a utilitarian perspective, the decision-maker should choose the option that will best serve the common good and give the highest sum of utility when all stakeholders are taken into account. Duty ethics can acknowledge some moral value to beneficial outcomes without accepting that they are reached through discrediting basic moral values like respect, dignity and honesty.

A utilitarian interpretation of the principle of equality considers what constitutes a morally relevant difference in terms of whether the options strengthen or weaken the pursuit of the common good. On this account, a decision-maker should consistently try to maximize utility for all concerned.

A duty ethics interpretation of the same principle would give weight to how the available options provide moral protection to the individuals involved and exemplify respect, dignity and honesty. Consistency from this ethical perspective is to always be respectful, transparent and honest in interactions with other stakeholders.

Of the two ethical perspectives, utilitarianism is the one most likely to find some positives in the choice of deleting the compromising photo. It would prompt the decision-maker to ask what good and bad can come out of disclosure and publicity of the HSE violation. If things can be dealt with more effectively with the photo out of the way, then utilitarian ethics would support that option. If, on the other hand, detection of the deletion of the photo is likely to cause scandal and misadventure for the involved parties, a utilitarian would change position accordingly.

Duty ethics, on the other hand, would be minimally concerned about outcomes and more interested in the extent to which the two options are examples of honesty and respectful behavior. It would thus be critical of the decision to conceal the mistakes that have occurred, both on the construction site and in the publication of the photo. Calculations of benefits are not part of the duty ethics repertory.

3   Principle of Publicity

A second ethical principle to guide decision-making highlights the value of being open and transparent about one's decisions and actions. Even here, Kant's moral philosophy has played a significant role in shaping conceptions about ethical justification. It draws a link between publicity and universality, claiming that what is public is, in principle, universally available for people to think about and more or less widely known. Ethical decision-making, by Kant's account, should be transparent and free of deception and misinformation. This concern can be translated into an action-guiding *principle of publicity*:

> Decision-makers should be willing to defend their decisions publicly and openly share their justifications with relevant stakeholders.

This line of thinking is behind various "front-page-of-a-newspaper" tests (Kvalnes, 2019). The advice to decision-makers is to consider whether they would be comfortable seeing their decision on the front page of *The New York Times* or another newspaper more relevant in their own context.

Going back to the Facebook case, the actual decision to delete a post with a compromising photo from the construction site is unlikely to pass the principle of publicity. "Deleted Facebook post with compromising photo" and "Ignored critical comments on HSE violation" are headlines that could easily have emerged in the local context where the story took place. One important clarification regarding the principle of publicity is that it should not be confused with a reputational principle. The question it poses is whether one would be willing to defend a decision publicly, not whether it is likely that one would actually have to do so. The latter reputational question would take into account the likelihood that anybody would detect or come to know about the decision. It is a characteristic feature of the ethical principle of publicity that it does not take into account the risk of detection. The likelihood that anybody would find out and leak to a news outlet may be zero, but the ethical requirement of publicity and transparency remains.

The principle of publicity makes little sense from a utilitarian perspective. Thinking about whether one would be willing to speak openly about one's decision does not in itself seem to add or distract from utility. If openness about one's pursuit of the common good could make more people understand and take up the utilitarian mindset, that would count as a positive thing, but otherwise there is no point to this thought experiment from a utilitarian point of view.

This utilitarian rejection of the principle does not mean that only decision-makers with duty ethics leanings can find it relevant. It is possible to be uncommitted to the conflict between the two normative traditions and still find it enlightening to consider one's options through the lens of this principle. If a person is hesitant or in doubt about whether he or she would be willing to justify a decision publicly, then it is a sign that this person considers the decision to be somewhat morally dubious.

With the principles of equality and publicity in place, we have a set of potentially action-guiding tools to apply when facing a dilemma in the use of social media. The next section introduces the Navigation Wheel, a model the decision-maker can use to keep track of a range of significant dimensions of the situation under consideration before making a decision. The model is primarily meant to guide the analytic process leading up to a decision but can also serve as a tool to consider the strengths and weaknesses of prior decisions and behavior.

4 The Navigation Wheel

The energizing flow of information and photos from a construction project came to a halt when a photo of an HSE violation was mistakenly posted on Facebook and spotted by users. The person running the Facebook account can (1) respond to the users' criticism before deleting the photo or (2) delete the photo without responding to the criticism. In the actual case, the decision-maker received desperate calls from the photographer and construction manager and quickly followed requests to delete the photo and get it out of the way before more damage could happen. This was a clear case of System 1 decision-making, and the current chapter takes a closer and slower look at the case, primarily to introduce a set of principles and questions to ask oneself during a System 2 process of reflectively figuring out what to do.

The extent to which responsible ethical behavior in organizations builds on System 1 or System 2 decision-making is open to discussion. Egorov, Verdorfer and Peus (2018) criticized the assumption that effective decision-making in business is primarily driven by conscious deliberation and analysis and proposed an inclusion of moral intuition as a constitutive part of responsible ethical behavior. They suggest that ethical deliberation and moral intuition should be seen as mutually supportive of each other, and the current study is aligned with that proposal. The main assumption here is that fast and intuitive decision-making is not sufficient in isolation but needs support from systematic deliberation.

Stenmark, Riley and Kreitler (2019) provided backing for that assumption. They found that people who learned a structured cognitive tool for decision-making performed better after an interruption than control groups on a number of markers of ethical decision-making and exhibited perceptions that they were better prepared to handle ethical dilemmas.

The Navigation Wheel is a cognitive tool that has been applied in organizational contexts since the beginning of the century. It was originally designed as a decision-making tool for leaders and employees participating in ethical training sessions (Kvalnes & Øverenget, 2012). Participants analyzed dilemmas in light of the six questions presented in the model (Fig. 3.1):

3 Ethical Navigation on Social Media 55

Fig. 3.1 The Navigation Wheel. (Source: Kvalnes, Ø., & Øverenget, E. (2012). Ethical navigation in leadership training. *Etikk i praksis—Nordic Journal of Applied Ethics* 6(1), 58–71)

The priority of questions in the model depends on context and is up to the decision-maker. The designers behind the Navigation Wheel did not envisage a particular order addressing the questions, and the relevance of each of them can vary with the situation.

The Navigation Wheel belongs to a family of models and question sets that propose a structure for analyses of dilemmas and other ethically challenging situations. One influential model is the ethical matrix (Mepham, 2000), designed to facilitate rational analysis of how decisions affect stakeholders in the domains of well-being, autonomy and justice. It has been applied in a range of contexts, including considerations of ethical challenges in agriculture (Kaiser, Millar, Thorstensen, & Tomkins, 2007), fishing (Kaiser & Forsberg, 2001), policy-making (Mepham, 2010) and technology (Kermisch & Depaus, 2018).

Alternative approaches suggest different sets of questions for the decision-maker to pose: "Is it legal, is it fair, can I defend it?" (Blanchard

& Peale, 1988) and "Why is this bothering me?—Who else matters?—Is it my problem?—What is the ethical concern?—What do others think?—Am I being true to myself?" (Rion, 1990). More complex approaches are described in van Luijk's 8-question list (2000), the 8-step list by Laczniak and Murphy (1985) and the 12-step list by Nash (1981).

A process involving the Navigation Wheel can start by identifying the most relevant options available and proceed by taking these options through the six questions in the model before using the answers and arguments that come out of that procedure as a foundation for making a decision.

Regarding LAW, the two options of (1) responding before deleting and (2) deleting without responding are both legally acceptable. There may be a legal obligation to report the HSE violation, but that is beyond the scope of the Facebook administrator's decision-making in this particular context. One noteworthy asymmetry when it comes to the legal aspect of the decision is that if an option is illegal, it constitutes a reason to refrain from choosing it, while if an option is legal, then that in itself does not constitute a reason for choosing it (Kvalnes & Øverenget, 2012). An agent may attempt to justify a decision by saying "it is legal to do it," but that is a weak argument, since the law in a country may allow many actions that one should refrain from for other reasons than legality.

IDENTITY in this analysis has to do with organizational and professional values. The decision-maker can ask "Is it in accordance with our values?" to choose the option under consideration. First, the organization may have defined a set of core values, which are action-guiding in the sense that they rule out certain options and recommend or even prohibit certain others. If the core values in a company are honesty and trust, these define the scope of action available to employees. Secondly, the decision-maker may belong to a particular profession where core values set the standard for what a person can and cannot do. Auditors are supposed to work from a platform of independence and objectivity; doctors and nurses are supposed to prioritize patients' interests ahead of their self-interests.

In the Facebook dilemma, we do not have information about the core values of the construction company. If they somehow highlight honesty, trust, transparency and openness, the decision-maker has strong reasons to reply properly to the critical messages to the post before deleting the photo. Core values may also be silent about communication with the public and so leave the decision-maker with freedom to choose between the two options.

When it comes to MORALITY, these are the moral beliefs and convictions of the decision-maker and the community that person belongs to. They manifest themselves in moral intuitions about the right course of action in a given situation. In the context of decision-making, the moral intuition may compete with other types of intuition and win or lose. During a process of deliberating about what to do, the moral aspect can come out in a reflection of whether it feels morally right or wrong to pursue a particular course of action.

The REPUTATION aspect of the decision has to do with how relevant stakeholders will respond in the event of finding out about the decision. If they are unlikely to ever receive information about it, the reputational risk is low. Here, the previously mentioned difference between the ethical principle of publicity and reputational concerns is important. The ethical question is whether one would be willing to defend the decision publicly, while the reputational question is whether one would actually have to do so. The latter question incorporates a deliberation about the risk of detection, which is not present in the former.

In the current case, the communications advisor knows that a decision to delete the photo will be known to a number of Facebook users. The reputational question she can consider is whether any of them will find it important enough to move forward with it. The HSE violation is a serious matter in light of how such violations have previously led to fatal accidents. The photo of an employee without a helmet and the subsequent deletion of the photo can be interpreted as an indication that the organization is failing to take the matter seriously. A concerned Facebook user thus has reasons to pursue the matter further. In the actual case, the decision was made very rapidly, apparently without much reflection, and may not have accounted for considerations of this kind.

ECONOMY is not a concern in the dilemma under scrutiny here, but it can be in other contexts. The options available to the decision-maker may put economic considerations up against ethical ones. The most profitable option may conflict with the organization's core values, and the choice may be between going bankrupt in an economic sense and with regard to identity. A dilemma can be a challenge to the integrity of a person, group or organization, in that it may pay off to flout one's own values on these three levels.

The final question in the Navigation Wheel is about ETHICS, which is where the ethical principles and theories from the previous section come in. The decision-maker can weigh his or her options by applying the principle of equality and considering which option is the most exemplary and the one to choose consistently in similar situations to the current one. That principle also encourages reflection on whether aspects of the situation warrant a break with a particular norm. "I would normally not delete content on Facebook before having replied to comments, but this situation was different" may be the introduction of a reflection pointing out morally relevant differences. When it comes to ethical theory, utilitarian ethics would accept a justification that could plausibly point to how deletion would maximize utility for the sum of stakeholders and would reject that course of action if the more plausible outcome is that stakeholders in sum would be worse off than with the alternative.

A decision-maker can (1) identify relevant options, (2) take each of them through a Navigation Wheel analysis and (3) make a decision based on that analysis. The model leaves open how to weight and prioritize the various aspects of the situation. What it does propose is a systematic way to analyze the available options and which set of questions one should take into consideration before making a decision. Justification of the decision can point back to the argumentation contained in the movement through the Navigation Wheel.

5 Ethical Debriefing

The primary purpose of the Navigation Wheel is to guide decision-making and provide a systematic framework for reflecting on available options and reaching an informed decision. It can also function as a tool for retrospective reflection about ethically challenging situations and the extent to which they are handled well. Ethical debriefing can strengthen individual and collective capabilities to cope with such situations in the future. Research from other areas of organizational life documents that experience in itself seldom leads to learning and enhancement of capabilities; it is a combination of experience and reflection that has the potential to do so (Di Stefano, Gino, Pisano, & Staats, 2016; Perusso, Blankesteijn, & Leal, 2019). The tradition of experiential learning theory elaborates on how knowledge is created through transformation of experience (Kolb, Boyatzis, & Mainemelis, 2001; Kolb & Yeganeh, 2011). It builds on Dewey's pragmatist philosophy and, more specifically, on the idea that deliberative restructuring of experience can add meaning to that experience and increase one's ability to direct the course of subsequent experience (Dewey, 1910). Ethical debriefing can take the form of analyzing the decision-making process to consider whether the most relevant and available options were given proper attention. Decision-makers can step away from the situation, take stock of their experience and articulate specific learning points to guide subsequent encounters with ethical dilemmas.

With the Navigation Wheel at hand, an ethical debriefing can consider the extent to which the process leading up to the decision considered the dimensions of law, identity, morality, reputation, economy and ethics for each of the alternatives. Did it neglect any of these dimensions? Which of them were particularly relevant to the decision at hand? In many situations, all the relevant alternatives are legal, so the question has never been whether one should break the law. In a well-functioning society, it is very seldom that an option to break the law comes under serious consideration in an organizational context. In those exceptional situations, the decision-maker considers civil disobedience or acting against the law for overriding moral reasons. For an example, see Kvalnes (2019, p. 52).

The reflection that constitutes an ethical debriefing can also consider the extent to which the decision under scrutiny was built on sufficient reflection or made in haste. In the main example of this chapter, it appears that the decision was built on fast System 1 thinking rather than on a slow System 2 process. One conclusion to come out of the debriefing can be that next time, one should take more time to consider the options at hand and take them through a Navigation Wheel type of analysis. Alternatively, one can conclude that future dilemmas are likely to come at a fast pace, demanding a quick and immediate response with limited time for ethical reflection. Under such circumstances, a possible organizational process can be to identify likely dilemmas upfront, in light of the categorization in this book or other frameworks, and then prepare for them in a slow, systematic and deliberate manner.

One factor that can stand in the way of constructive ethical debriefing is the human propensity to let actual outcomes dominate retrospective reflections and judgments. If things have turned out well, it is tempting to conclude that the ethical decision-making has been exemplary. On the other hand, if things have turned out badly, the tendency may be to think that there must have been some ethical flaws in the reasoning leading up to the decision. The concept of moral luck was mentioned in the previous chapter in connection with tempo dilemmas. The higher the tempo, the more likely that a decision will be flawed and have unwelcome consequences. Here, the concept of moral luck can serve to warn against a tendency to let actual outcomes color the moral judgment of decisions and actions, even in situations in which elements beyond the agent's control have been decisive (Nagel, 1979; Williams, 1981). Theoretically, we may think that a person should only be morally judged by what is within his or her control, but that conviction often disappears in real-life contexts, where the actual outcome takes center stage.

Moral luck constitutes a trap for those who aim to learn from their previous behavior in an ethically challenging situation. On the one hand, they may mistakenly reason that since the outcome was good, they handled the situation well. In reality, they may have simply have had good moral luck, in that a fortunate set of circumstances led to an outcome in which no one was harmed. On the other hand, bad moral luck can lead decision-makers to mistakenly reason that their initial decision was irresponsible and unethical, when in fact they have been victims of an unfortunate set of circumstances. A decision based on a reasonable risk can sometimes lead to a negative outcome, while a decision based on an unreasonable risk can lead to a positive (or at least not negative) outcome. Learning processes should focus on the situation as it was ahead of the decision and what the agents knew or were in a position to know at that time rather than on haphazard outcomes.

Empirical studies demonstrate that unlucky decision-makers are indeed judged more harshly with regard to the moral quality of their actions than lucky ones (Martin & Cushman, 2016). A drunk driver who hits and injures a pedestrian is judged more harshly than a drunk driver who happens to not hurt anybody. A rescue attempt is held in higher moral regard if it is successful than if it is not, even if the difference between the two attempts are solely due to uncontrollable circumstances. The pattern is likely to hold even in social media contexts. An executive may have posted a harsh message on Twitter that would have received moral criticism if a critical world event had not occurred at the same time and took her followers' full attention. However, research also indicates that the moral difference between lucky and unlucky decision-makers and agents tends to disappear with reflection (Kneer & Machery, 2019). Through reflection, we have the capacity to overcome what Royzman and Kumar (2004) have called epistemically corrupt evaluations. This means that a reflective and honest ethical debriefing can lead decision-makers away from the moral luck trap to a realistic understanding of what has taken place and the extent to which the situation has been handled in an exemplary way.

This chapter has presented a model for analyzing options when facing a dilemma at work involving aspects of law, identity, morality, reputation, economy and ethics. The Navigation Wheel can provide support for a slow and reflective approach to such situations, in contrast to the fast and intuitive one that often manifests itself in organizational contexts. The approach has here been exemplified through an analysis of a social media dilemma in which the decision-maker was a Facebook administrator for a company and had to find a way out of a challenging situation. We have also seen that the Navigation Wheel can have a purpose in retrospective processes and serve to structure ethical debriefing, in which the aim is to articulate the experience and reflect on it in order to learn and improve one's handling of ethical dilemmas.

Many of the executive students who contributed to the categorization of dilemmas in this study expressed concerns regarding the resources available to them when facing stressful and demanding dilemmas. Limited leadership support and a lack of guiding norms and principles put them in precarious situations where impulse and intuition often dominate over more thoughtful responses. Ethical training and familiarity with the Navigation Wheel and similar tools have the potential to make them better prepared for coping with ethical dilemmas on social media.

The topic of the next and final chapter is leadership and social media. The starting point is the frustration expressed by many informants regarding a lack of sufficient support from their leaders when facing ethical dilemmas. It proceeds by discussing that frustration in light of the concepts of ethical leadership and balanced leadership before ending with a proposal to research and study ethics on social media through the lens of a distinction between do-good ethics and avoid-harm ethics.

References

Blanchard, K., & Peale, N. V. (1988). *The power of ethical management*. New York: William Morrow and Company. In: Inc.

Dewey, J. (1910). *How we think*. Boston, MA: D. C. Heath.

Di Stefano, G., Gino, F., Pisano, G. P., & Staats, B. R. (2016). *Making experience count: The role of reflection in individual learning*. Harvard Business School NOM Unit Working Paper (14–093), 14–093.

Egorov, M., Verdorfer, A. P., & Peus, C. (2018). Taming the emotional dog: Moral intuition and ethically-oriented leader development. *Journal of Business Ethics, 160*(3), 1–18.

Kahneman, D. (2013). *Thinking, fast and slow*. New York: Farrar, Straus and Giroux.

Kaiser, M., & Forsberg, E.-M. (2001). Assessing fisheries–using an ethical matrix in a participatory process. *Journal of Agricultural and Environmental Ethics, 14*(2), 191–200.

Kaiser, M., Millar, K., Thorstensen, E., & Tomkins, S. (2007). Developing the ethical matrix as a decision support framework: GM fish as a case study. *Journal of Agricultural and Environmental Ethics, 20*(1), 65–80.

Kant, I. (1983). *Kant's ethical philosophy*. Indianapolis: Hacking Publishing Company.

Kant, I. (1998 (1785)). *Groundwork of the Metaphysics of Morals* (M. Gregor Ed.). New York: Cambridge University Press.

Kermisch, C., & Depaus, C. (2018). The strength of ethical matrixes as a tool for normative analysis related to technological choices: The case of geological disposal for radioactive waste. *Science and Engineering Ethics, 24*(1), 29–48.

Kneer, M., & Machery, E. (2019). No luck for moral luck. *Cognition, 182*, 331–348.

Kolb, D. A., Boyatzis, R. E., & Mainemelis, C. (2001). Experiential learning theory: Previous research and new directions. *Perspectives on thinking, learning, and cognitive styles, 1*(8), 227–247.

Kolb, D. A., & Yeganeh, B. (2011). Deliberate experiential learning: Mastering the art of learning from experience. In K. Elsbach, D. C. Kayes, & A. Kayes (Eds.), *Contemporary organizational behavior in action*. London: Pearson.

Kvalnes, Ø. (2019). *Moral reasoning at work: Rethinking ethics in organizations* (2nd ed.). London: Palgrave Macmillan.

Kvalnes, Ø., & Øverenget, E. (2012). Ethical navigation in leadership training. *Etikk i praksis-Nordic Journal of Applied Ethics, 6*(1), 58–71.

Laczniak, G. R., & Murphy, P. E. (1985). *Marketing ethics: Guidelines for managers*. Lexington, MA: Lexington Books.

Martin, J. W., & Cushman, F. (2016). The adaptive logic of moral luck. *The Blackwell Companion to Experimental Philosophy*, 190–202.

Mepham, B. (2000). A framework for the ethical analysis of novel foods: The ethical matrix. *Journal of Agricultural and Environmental Ethics, 12*(2), 165–176.

Mepham, B. (2010). The ethical matrix as a tool in policy interventions: The obesity crisis. In *Food ethics* (pp. 17–29). New York: Springer.

Nagel, T. (1979). *Moral luck. In Mortal questions*. Cambridge: Cambridge University Press.

Nash, L. L. (1981). Ethics without the sermon. *Harvard Business Review, 59*(6), 79–90.

Perusso, A., Blankesteijn, M., & Leal, R. (2019). The contribution of reflective learning to experiential learning in business education. *Assessment & Evaluation in Higher Education*, 1–15.

Rion, M. (1990). *The responsible manager*. San Francisco: Harper & Row.

Royzman, E., & Kumar, R. (2004). Is consequential luck morally inconsequential? Empirical psychology and the reassessment of moral luck. *Ratio, 17*(3), 329–344.

Stenmark, C., Riley, K., & Kreitler, C. (2019). Ethical decision-making interrupted: Can cognitive tools improve decision-making following an interruption? *Ethics & Behavior*, 1–24.

Van Luijk, H. J. L. (2000). In search of instruments. Business and ethics halfway. In *Business challenging business ethics: New instruments for coping with diversity in international business* (pp. 3–8). New York: Springer.

Wattles, J. (1996). *The Golden rule*. New York: Oxford University Press.
Williams, B. (1981). *Moral luck: Philosophical papers 1973–1980*. Cambridge: Cambridge University Press.

Open Access This chapter is licensed under the terms of the Creative Commons Attribution 4.0 International License (http://creativecommons.org/licenses/by/4.0/), which permits use, sharing, adaptation, distribution and reproduction in any medium or format, as long as you give appropriate credit to the original author(s) and the source, provide a link to the Creative Commons licence and indicate if changes were made.

The images or other third party material in this chapter are included in the chapter's Creative Commons licence, unless indicated otherwise in a credit line to the material. If material is not included in the chapter's Creative Commons licence and your intended use is not permitted by statutory regulation or exceeds the permitted use, you will need to obtain permission directly from the copyright holder.

4

Leadership and Ethics in Social Media

Abstract This chapter discusses leadership dimensions of social media ethics through the lens of theories about ethical leadership and balanced leadership. Informants within this study have reported about (1) insufficient support from leaders, who tend to have restricted understanding of the workings of social media; (2) a lack of established codes or norms; (3) an absence of narratives about exemplary handlings of previous cases; and (4) limited access to concepts and ideas to clarify the issues at stake. Categorization of ethical dilemmas that occur in connection with social media use can potentially bring employees and leaders closer together in a common understanding of the challenges. The Navigation Wheel and related principles can be helpful for thinking systematically about the alternatives at hand and in ethical debriefings. The chapter ends with a reflection on how ethics with regard to social media has a proscriptive (avoid harm) and prescriptive (do good) dimension.

Keywords Ethical leadership • Balanced leadership • Social media • Proscriptive ethics • Prescriptive ethics

A bank wanted to reach out to younger people and asked two employees from that generation to come up with a humorous narrative that could be conveyed through photos on Instagram. The employees responded to the challenge by creating a story about a 23-year-old man who was using his credit card to live an active and adventurous life. They made a fictitious account on Instagram and posted photos of the credit card in various contexts. The young man used it in everyday situations, travelling and enjoying himself with friends. To get more attention, though, the narrative gradually became more controversial and daring. The young man attended a German Oktoberfest, where his credit card was photographed placed in the cleavage of a woman serving beer in a local costume. In his travel to Amsterdam, he was shown peeking through the window of a brothel, credit card in hand. Another photo showed the logo of a clinic known for treating sexually transmitted diseases. The story of the young credit card user was meant to be lighthearted, humorous and appealing to a younger generation of bank customers, but now negative reactions began to appear. Both older people and representatives of the target generation criticized the Instagram marketing for exhibiting sexism and male chauvinism. The most provocative photos were quickly deleted, and after a while, the bank terminated the story of the young credit card user.

The marketing director of the bank was one of the executive students who contributed to the categorization of digital dilemmas in this study. He explained in class how negative responses to the Instagram narrative put the leadership of the organization to the test. Clearly, the people responsible for the postings had gone too far and put the bank in a difficult situation. They had faced a tempo dilemma; how were they to keep up the intensity and pace of this particular story? In hindsight, their decision-making was ethically flawed. Put in Navigation Wheel terms, the Instagram story raised questions about the bank's identity and core values, creating a minor reputational crisis. This was an old, traditional organization associated with social responsibility and a stable set of values. From an ethical point of view, the posting of the photos was also questionable because they promoted a view of the female body as a commodity for rich men. However, the two employees had been given a scope of action for experimenting with and testing ideas in a high-tempo format. Leaders at the bank protected them from public criticism and took responsibility for any offense the campaign caused.

The final chapter of this book addresses social media ethics in relation to leadership. The use of social media in organizational contexts creates ethical challenges for leaders, as illustrated by the case of the Instagram postings described above. In that particular scenario, the leaders took responsibility and offered protection to employees who had overstepped the boundaries of ethical social media use. The input to this study indicates that this kind of ethically appropriate leadership in a social media context is rare. Leaders struggle to cope adequately in such situations, particularly if they are unfamiliar with the workings of social media.

The first section addresses how informants report on an absence of what research has labeled ethical leadership (Brown, Treviño, & Harrison, 2005), that is, normatively appropriate conduct through personal actions and interpersonal relationships. The informants are professionals responsible for handling the social media platforms for their organizations. When they face ethical dilemmas, they seek ethical guidance and support from their leaders. In response, these leaders tend to expect the informants to be the experts, not only on the workings of social media but also on appropriate responses to ethically questionable behavior among colleagues or other ethical issues arising from social media use. Additionally, some informants report that the leaders themselves engage in unethical behavior on social media. An absence of ethical leadership thus appears to restrict social media professionals' ability to cope with ethical dilemmas at work.

The second section applies the concept of balanced leadership and explores how it can shed light on the tensions reported by informants in relation to leaders in their organizations. Balanced leadership derives from a combination of vertical leadership, which is an activity performed by one person overlooking and instructing processes in an organization, and horizontal leadership, which takes place between members of a team and alternates between them (Müller, Packendorff, & Sankaran, 2017). Leaders with a restricted understanding of the nature of social media are ill equipped to exercise vertical leadership in the sense of offering support or guidance when ethical dilemmas appear. An organization can address this problem by creating opportunities for leaders to learn more about social media, by opening up horizontal leadership, whereunder the responsibility for taking initiatives and supporting colleagues lies with each member of the team, or by a combination of these options.

The final section of this chapter outlines how social media create ethical issues connected not only to the avoidance of negative behaviors and outcomes, but also to the promotion of positive ones. Familiarity with the distinction between do-good ethics and avoid-harm ethics in the realm of social media should belong to the vocabulary of leaders. Organizational ethics has a tendency to focus on the harmful aspects of agency and decision-making at the expense of the beneficial aspects. Ethics has largely been associated with the kinds of behaviors one should avoid, rather than those kinds one should practice to bring about positive change. The do not's have dominated over the do's and the should not's over the should's. Research has identified this asymmetry and called for more attention to the ethics of doing good (Janoff-Bulman, Sheikh, & Hepp, 2009; Mayer, 2010; Treviño, Weaver, & Reynolds, 2006). The current study ends with a reflection on how practitioners and researchers with an ethics orientation should have their eyes open to both the harmful and the beneficial aspects of social media.

1 Ethical Leadership

The concept of ethical leadership has been defined as a demonstration of normatively appropriate conduct through personal actions and interpersonal relationships, with an emphasis on the promotion of such conduct to followers through two-way communication, reinforcement and decision-making (Brown et al., 2005; Neubert, Carlson, Kacmar, Roberts, & Chonko, 2009). In the opening example, the leaders in the bank appear to have responded to the ethical challenges connected to the provocative Instagram postings in an exemplary manner. They demonstrated normatively appropriate conduct by shielding from criticism the employees who had been given a scope of action for experimenting with the format.

The high tempo of social media increases the risk of making mistakes, which is a significant challenge for normatively appropriate leadership practices in the area. As noted in previous chapters, the concept of moral luck describes how actual outcomes affect moral judgments on decisions and actions, even when they are affected by factors beyond an agent's control (Nagel, 1979; Williams, 1981). Fear of moral luck can lead professionals on social media and in other settings to experience moral paralysis (Kvalnes, 2017), a reluctance to take any form of risk due to a perceived lack of protection against criticism and repercussions if the outcome of one's efforts should happen to be unwelcome or bad. In a social media context, leaders can prevent moral paralysis by being supportive of their employees when they engage in risky activities. Their commitment and support are put to the test when high-tempo experimentation actually causes harm, as in the Oktoberfest Instagram story outlined above. In that particular case, the leaders displayed ethical leadership by taking responsibility and providing adequate protection to the employees involved. Input from this study's informants indicates that ethical leadership of this kind is exceptional. They report an absence of such leadership, as leaders' self-interest apparently dominates over concern for what is best for an organization.

Leadership is put to the test in interactions between social media specialists and their leaders. Based on input to this study, it appears that the leaders tend to withdraw from challenges at hand and leave the responsibility to the social media professionals. Here is one example from the student memos:

> We had a managerial vacancy in my organization and wanted to recruit internally. Three candidates applied for the position. One of the candidates who did not get the position thought that she had been treated unfairly and discriminated against based on gender. We have a male-dominated management group, and the candidate who got the job is a man. The woman who felt badly treated took out her frustration on her Facebook page and thereby reached a wide audience within and outside our organization. I received a message from top management requesting that I should talk to the employee and get her to delete the posts and find other ways of communicating her grievances. I was very uncomfortable with that request. Was it really my responsibility to address the issue with the employee? I am responsible for the social media accounts in our organization and know

more about social media than the people in the management group do. Even so, you do not need to be a specialist in the workings of social media to explain to an employee that she has stepped over the line. To me, it seemed natural that her nearest manager should have that difficult conversation with her.

This example is one of several where the informants—people who run social media platforms for an organization—have felt that they are expected to step into leadership roles. They face role confusion and ultimately role dilemmas. Their main responsibility is to administer and optimize social media use for their organizations, but when human resources issues like the one described above occur, they are expected to take initiative there as well. The informants then typically respond with frustration, since they lack a formal leadership role. Taking on leadership responsibilities is not part of their job descriptions, and they do not have the authority to dispense specific instructions on ethical aspects of social media use. They may be in a position to say, "Your/my/our leader told me to tell you," but that in itself begs the question of why a leader is not present in the conversation.

Another typical situation is one where leaders push for a particular message to be published though an organization's social media but lack the expertise to judge the wisdom of doing so:

> My leaders have different meanings about what we should publish digitally and are trying to promote their messages on social media. Everybody thinks that his or her message is the most important one. So far we have no strategy regarding what to publish, but I have a relatively good grasp of what works well and what does not work. Should I refuse my superiors to publish what I think would reflect badly on them and our organization, or let them publish whatever they want?

This situation seems to constitute a false dilemma, since it would be wrong to let the leaders publish whatever they want. It appears that social media professionals should intervene and stop social media use that could reflect poorly on the leader and the organization. However, in such cases, it is difficult and risky to do the ethically right thing because criticism of a leader's behavior on social media may not be a good career move. Regardless, leaders who insist on the primacy of their own messages fail to exemplify normatively appropriate conduct and as such fall short of the requirements of ethical leadership.

Ethical leaders are fair, honest and principled individuals who use various forms of rewards, punishments and communication mechanisms to influence their followers' ethical behavior. A range of studies have documented that ethical leadership tends to create positive follower outcomes (Bedi, Alpaslan, & Green, 2016). Research has suggested that ethical leadership boosts psychological well-being and job satisfaction (Avey, Wernsing, & Palanski, 2012) as well as trust (Brown et al., 2005), and that it decreases employees' propensity to morally disengage (Moore et al., 2019). Organizations thus have multiple reasons to recruit and develop people who can exercise ethical leadership.

The research on ethical leadership has suggested that much can be gained from promoting and displaying it and that there are corresponding downsides to its absence. One of the examples discussed under the heading of speech dilemmas in Chap. 2 can serve as an illustration of leadership that is lacking in ethical quality:

> I am working for a public directorate. The minster has initiated dramatic changes in our procedures. One of my colleagues is very critical to these changes based on his expertise and experience. He uses Twitter to express his criticism of the minister's initiative and receives so much attention that even the non-digital management in the directorate gets to hear about it. Now they ask me, as a representative of the communications unit, to tell the colleague to stop using Twitter to express his critical views. How should I proceed?

This social media professional is understandably ill at ease at the prospect of being handed the responsibility to intervene in a colleague's Twitter use. It poses a role dilemma in that the professional feels that he and his management are operating from conflicting understandings of their designated roles. It also has an integrity dilemma dimension, as the agent would compromise his professional standards if he were to obey the order from management. The outspoken employee faced a speech dilemma—can I use Twitter in this manner?—and his decision creates a dilemma in the same category for the social media professional and his leaders. What are they entitled to say now, from an ethical point of view?

The situation is parallel to the one outlined at the beginning of the chapter, wherein an employee was using Facebook to complain about perceived unfair treatment in an internal recruitment process. Active and engaged leadership in neither case requires expertise in the specific workings of social media. The colleague's leader should be perfectly capable of addressing the issue with the employee, even without a grasp of how Twitter works. If the matter is considered to be serious, then surely the message should come from a leader. A leader who refuses to deliver the said message fails to engage in ethical leadership in terms of taking personal action and showing normatively appropriate behavior.

Many of the informants in this study express similar frustration over what can be deemed a lack of exemplary, ethical leadership from their superiors. The leaders typically push the responsibility for handling ethical dilemmas onto the social media professionals. The more overarching problem that informants report is a lack of resources for appropriate handling of ethical dilemmas. They are entering unfamiliar technological territory, where ethical navigation is difficult due to a number of factors:

1. Insufficient support from leaders, who tend to have restricted understanding of the workings of social media
2. A lack of established codes or norms
3. An absence of narratives about exemplary handlings of previous cases
4. Limited access to concepts and ideas that clarify the issues at stake

The current study offers potential for release from the first and last of these frustrations. The proposed categorization of dilemmas can serve to bring practitioners and their leaders closer together. It identifies the kinds of situations that can occur in connection with social media use in organizations and thus provides a common platform from which to draw up plans and strategies for handling them in a constructive manner. With the introduction of the Navigation Wheel and ethical principles, it also provides a common platform for reflection on the dilemmas.

Ethical leadership does not require expertise in every professional dimension of what goes on in an organization. More specifically, a leader can act in a principled, honest and fair manner when a dilemma on social media occurs in an organization. Lack of detailed knowledge about the workings of Facebook or Twitter is no excuse for stepping back from potentially toxic situations, where a person or group handling social media communication for an organization is seeking support to resolve an ethical dilemma. One way to offer support can be to join in a discussion about alternative options, a systematic analysis whereby the participants seek out a solution together. If somebody within an organization is judged to have misused social media, it seems reasonable for a leader to address that misuse with the person involved and not delegate the responsibility to individuals in charge of social media accounts.

2 Balanced Leadership

The informants of this study report a recurring pattern of cases where a senior employee or leader has developed bad habits in using social media, either on behalf of the organization or in a capacity that can easily be associated with the organization. The impulsive and thoughtless posts on Facebook are there for all to see. The informants convey that in such situations, their leaders expect them—the social media experts—to address the issue with the employee or leader. The previous section discussed requests of this kind under the heading of ethical leadership, defined as a demonstration of normatively appropriate conduct through personal actions and interpersonal relationships. It argued that it is unreasonable of leaders to order social media professionals to step into their shoes to perform leadership tasks.

At first glance, it appears that leaders who delegate difficult conversations with employees about questionable Facebook use onto subordinates thereby neglect their leadership responsibilities. It seems reasonable to assume that a leader's responsibilities typically include handling human relations issues that arise from ethical aspects of social media use in the organization. Building up an understanding of the workings of social media should be an important priority for people with leadership ambitions in organizations where Facebook and other platforms are likely to be central to communication with stakeholders.

Another interpretation of the leadership behaviors reported in this study is that some of them are invitations to lead, rather than neglect of one's own responsibilities. The formal leaders appear to be inviting social media professionals to engage in distributed leadership (Spillane & Diamond, 2007), as if they are saying, "Here is a critical situation at work, and now you can take the lead in resolving it." Such leaders provide professionals under their command with a scope of action for taking the lead. It is common to view leadership as an activity performed by one person—the leader—but it can also be useful to consider it as an ongoing activity executed between members of a team. In daily activities, the members can take turns being the leader. The distinction between vertical and horizontal leadership brings out this difference (Müller et al., 2018). In a range of organizational settings, the role of setting standards, motivating colleagues and keeping a project on track does not belong to one person who vertically oversees and manages the processes; instead, team members alternate on taking the lead. Studies on project management have identified the need to establish balanced leadership, which allows for vertical and horizontal leadership simultaneously (Müller et al., 2017).

The need for balanced leadership is evident in cases where ethical issues on social media occur within an organization and there are no formal leadership structures in place to address or resolve them. Somebody needs to take initiative, and social media professionals may not even be aware of the issue at hand. In such circumstances, an organization open to horizontal leadership is less vulnerable to mishaps, as it is normal for people other than the vertically placed leaders to intervene and attend to the matter at hand.

Social media creates a platform for rapid exchange of information, and as noted previously, this high tempo increases the likelihood of mishaps and blunders. If the person at the keyboard is also under the influence of alcohol or other substances, the probability of embarrassment is even higher. One informant described a situation where a senior, high-profile person in an organization was active on Twitter one Friday evening and appeared to be drunk. She was using rude and expressive language in dialogue with other Twitter users. Whose responsibility was it to take action and stop her from further embarrassing herself and the organization? This was a situation where somebody, either a fellow manager or someone lower in the organization, needed to take initiative to halt the turn of events. An organization depends on a scope of action for taking the lead beyond rank and hierarchy to cope with such situations.

One challenge obstructing positive outcomes to situations where a drunk representative of an organization is active on social media is the psychological phenomenon called the bystander effect (Darley & Latané, 1968; Latané & Darley, 1976). A diffusion of responsibility can occur when many people are witnesses to a critical situation. Furthermore, when many bystanders are present and people observe that nobody is taking action, that perception can lead to pluralistic ignorance—a sense that because others are passive, there is little cause for alarm (Beu, Buckley, & Harvey, 2000; Zhu & Westphal, 2011). For a discussion of the relevance of the bystander effect for ethics, see Kvalnes (2019).

These reflections on horizontal leadership as a supplement to vertical leadership are not meant as corrections to the frustrations of this study's informants, who have experienced leaders unreasonably pushing leadership responsibilities onto them. The informants' examples appear to come from organizations with vertical leadership structures, whereby it is the leaders' responsibility to discipline employees, even when they misbehave in a format and context on which the leader lacks adequate understanding. The point of discussing balanced leadership is rather to highlight that dilemmas stemming from social media use in organizations may be dealt with more adequately if horizontal structures are established as supplements to the more traditional, person-oriented, vertical structures.

Leadership in connection with social media is an area that deserves further attention from researchers and practitioners. Ethical dilemmas are among the key challenges that leaders and employees need to cope with together. The categorizations and analytical tools in this book provide a platform for doing so in a systematic manner, to avoid being solely reliant on fast and intuitive decision-making.

3 Doing Good and Avoiding Harm

The aim of the final section of this book is to convey the breadth of issues that fall under the heading of ethics in the context of digital transformation and social media. Leaders and other decision-makers should be aware that ethics is concerned not only with avoiding harm, but also with doing good. In organizational ethics, people have been guilty of emphasizing the former at the expense of the latter. The do not's and the should not's have prevailed over the do's and should's. Researchers have noted this asymmetry and called for a more balanced presentation of ethical issues, one that clearly acknowledges that ethical concerns and responsibilities include both avoiding negative behaviors and outcomes and promoting positive ones (Carnes & Janoff-Bulman, 2012; Janoff-Bulman et al., 2009; Sheikh & Janoff-Bulman, 2010; Treviño et al., 2006).

Calls for a symmetrical view of ethics, giving attention to doing good and not just avoiding harm, have parallels in the domains of psychology and organizational studies. The emergence of positive psychology came as a response to decades of extensive research on anxiety and depression and of relatively little attention to joy and well-being. It generated a shift in attention from pathological psychological states to optimal ones (Seligman, 2002; Sheldon & King, 2001). Similarly, positive organizational scholarship shifted the focus from conflict, stress, burnout and other negative aspects of working life to what characterizes organizations that nurture human strength and resilience in employees, make restoration and reconciliation possible and cultivate extraordinary individual and organizational performance (Cameron & Dutton, 2003; Cameron, Dutton, & Quinn, 2003; Dutton, 2003).

Organizational ethics has needed a similar change in focus, from the dark sides to the bright sides of human interaction and from the ways leaders and employees misbehave in organizational settings to how individual and collaborative efforts from prosocial motives can generate positive outcomes.

The distinction between do-good ethics and avoid-harm ethics is highly relevant in the context of social media. Here there is also a risk of emphasizing the avoidance aspects of ethics over the good things that can

Table 4.1 Do-good and avoid-harm ethics issues in social media

Do-good ethics	Social media use should contribute to the following: • Empowerment • Transparency • Employee engagement • Sharing of knowledge • Driving positive change • Prosocial behavior
Avoid-harm ethics	Social media use should not contribute to the following: • Loss of integrity • Harassment • Discrimination • Trolling • Fake news • Destructive politics

come out of social media use in organizations. There are ethical traps one should avoid, by not posting certain kinds of content, not sacrificing one's integrity, not exploiting one's superior competence to trick a client and so on. A long list of such do not's and should not's can overshadow ethically positive uses of social media. An alternative starting point can be to list general ethical issues in the two domains (Table 4.1):

The items in these lists are preliminary suggestions for what could belong under the two headings, and more can be added to both categories. Emerging research has provided content for the positive ethical dimensions of social media. Ewing, Men, and O'Neil (2019) studied how internal use of social media in organizations can engage and empower employees. Social media create a platform for sharing knowledge within organizations (Havakhor, Soror, & Sabherwal, 2018; Neeley & Leonardi, 2018). Proper use of social media can help form smart organizations characterized by a free flow of information and shared knowledge (Nisar, Prabhakar, & Strakova, 2019).

Positive and constructive aspects of organizational social media use are not normally placed under the heading of ethics. The phenomena may be acknowledged but are not framed as having anything to do with ethics in a given organization. However, the shift in attention within organizational ethics suggests that these beneficial aspects belong in that framework when taking stock of the ethical dimensions of social media. Habits and patterns of understanding ethics primarily through avoidance of negative behaviors and outcomes are hard to dispel. Their source may be the general phenomenon of negativity bias, which is the human propensity to give more attention to the negative aspects of bad outcomes than to the positive aspects of good outcomes (Tversky & Kahneman, 1991; Vaish, Grossmann, & Woodward, 2008). The negativity pattern is present even in the informants' input. They were not introduced to the difference between do-good ethics and avoid-harm ethics in advance of making their contributions, and a pattern emerges in the material of seeing that their ethical challenges mainly involve avoidance of negative behaviors and outcomes. This can be regarded as a limitation of the study. Giving the students directions on the difference between the two ethics types and how organizational ethics encompasses both may have provided more variation and breadth in their input, as well as material for a more symmetrical account of ethical dilemmas in handling organizations' social media platforms.

Future studies of ethical dilemmas in social media use can incorporate the distinction between do-good ethics and avoid-harm ethics. On a general note, it seems that ethical dilemmas can materialize when a decision-maker must prioritize between two possible positive outcomes or when the only way to reach a positive outcome appears to be through behaviors that are negative. Many ethical do-good projects can be pursued without creating conflict by either of these considerations. In such ethically harmonious and tension-free circumstances, constructive use of social media can energize an organization and bring about positive change.

This final chapter has connected ethics on social media to leadership. The opening example was one where posting provocative photos on Instagram led to public criticism of a bank. The leadership intervened in what appeared to be an ethically exemplary manner, by protecting the employees who had posted the photos and taking responsibility. Input to the current study indicates that leaders in organizations struggle to cope with the ethical challenges raised by social media use. Many of the informants have expressed frustration over a lack of leadership support in dealing with ethical dilemmas. What they have found wanting can be labeled ethical leadership, which is understood as normatively appropriate behavior based on personal actions and interpersonal relationships. From the informants' perspectives, their leaders have not been sufficiently present as principled, honest and fair supporters when ethical dilemmas have occurred. The examples seem to have come from organizations with predominantly vertical leadership structures, and one remedy suggested here has been to introduce horizontal leadership, which takes place between members of a team. Under such leadership, the responsibilities to intervene, offer support and raise critical questions lie with each member. Balanced leadership happens when there is a combination of vertical and horizontal leadership in an organization. Constructive development of social media use in an organization seems to depend on the presence of horizontal leadership, either as the main way of leading or in tandem with vertical leadership.

The final section presented the distinction between do-good ethics and avoid-harm ethics as crucial for developing symmetrical organizational ethics and mapping the breadth of ethical issues produced by social media. This distinction is necessary to acknowledge the ethically positive aspects of social media.

Inspiration to write this book came from encounters with engaged practitioners whose day-to-day working lives consist of administrating social media accounts on behalf of their organizations. Over a period of five years, executive students who belong to this category of employees have generously shared their experiences and allowed their memos to form the data for this study. From the outset, the ambition of the book has been to come up with a theory that can be of use to practitioners. The categorization and cognitive tools conveyed in it can support and enhance ethically responsible decision-making and behavior in the use of social media. The book thus reaches out to practitioners with organizational roles similar to the ones of those who have contributed to the study. Fellow academics may also find elements here that they would like to expand on and elaborate further in the name of research.

References

Avey, J. B., Wernsing, T. S., & Palanski, M. E. (2012). Exploring the process of ethical leadership: The mediating role of employee voice and psychological ownership. *Journal of Business Ethics, 107*(1), 21–34.

Bedi, A., Alpaslan, C. M., & Green, S. (2016). A meta-analytic review of ethical leadership outcomes and moderators. *Journal of Business Ethics, 139*(3), 517–536.

Beu, D. S., Buckley, M. R., & Harvey, M. G. (2000). The role of pluralistic ignorance in the perception of unethical behavior. *Journal of Business Ethics, 23*(4), 353–364.

Brown, M. E., Treviño, L. K., & Harrison, D. A. (2005). Ethical leadership: A social learning perspective for construct development and testing. *Organizational Behavior and Human Decision Processes, 97*(2), 117–134.

Cameron, K., & Dutton, J. (2003). *Positive organizational scholarship: Foundations of a new discipline.* San Francisco, CA: Berrett-Koehler Publishers.

Cameron, K., Dutton, J., & Quinn, R. (2003). An introduction to positive organizational scholarship. *Positive organizational scholarship, 3,* 13.

Carnes, N., & Janoff-Bulman, R. (2012). Harm, help, and the nature of (im)moral (in) action. *Psychological Inquiry, 23*(2), 137–142.

Darley, J. M., & Latané, B. (1968). Bystander intervention in emergencies: Diffusion of responsibility. *Journal of Personality and Social Psychology, 8*(4), 377–383.

Dutton, J. (2003). *Energize your workplace: How to create and sustain high-quality connections at work.* New York: John Wiley & Sons.

Ewing, M., Men, L. R., & O'Neil, J. (2019). Using social media to engage employees: Insights from internal communication managers. *International Journal of Strategic Communication, 13*(2), 110–132.

Havakhor, T., Soror, A. A., & Sabherwal, R. (2018). Diffusion of knowledge in social media networks: Effects of reputation mechanisms and distribution of knowledge roles. *Information Systems Journal, 28*(1), 104–141.

Janoff-Bulman, R., Sheikh, S., & Hepp, S. (2009). Proscriptive versus prescriptive morality: Two faces of moral regulation. *Journal of Personality and Social Psychology, 96*(3), 521.

Kvalnes, Ø. (2017). *Fallibility at work: Rethinking excellence and error in organizations.* London: Palgrave Macmillan.

Kvalnes, Ø. (2019). *Moral reasoning at work: Rethinking ethics in organizations* (2nd ed.). London: Palgrave Macmillan.

Latané, B., & Darley, J. M. (1976). *Help in a crisis: Bystander response to an emergency.* Morriston, NJ: General Learning Press.

Mayer, D. M. (2010). From proscriptions to prescriptions: A call for including prosocial behavior in behavioral ethics. In *Managerial ethics. Managing the psychology of morality* (pp. 257–269). New York: Routledge.

Moore, C., Mayer, D. M., Chiang, F. F., Crossley, C., Karlesky, M. J., & Birtch, T. A. (2019). Leaders matter morally: The role of ethical leadership in shaping employee moral cognition and misconduct. *Journal of Applied Psychology, 104*(1), 123.

Müller, R., Packendorff, J., & Sankaran, S. (2017). Balanced leadership: A new perspective for leadership in organizational project management. In S. Sankaran, R. Müller, & N. Drouin (Eds.), *Cambridge handbook of organizational project management.* Cambridge: Cambridge University Press

Müller, R., Sankaran, S., Drouin, N., Vaagaasar, A.-L., Bekker, M. C., & Jain, K. (2018). A theory framework for balancing vertical and horizontal leadership in projects. *International Journal of Project Management, 36*(1), 83–94.

Nagel, T. (1979). Moral luck. In *Mortal questions.* Cambridge: Cambridge University Press.

Neeley, T. B., & Leonardi, P. M. (2018). Enacting knowledge strategy through social media: P assable trust and the paradox of nonwork interactions. *Strategic Management Journal, 39*(3), 922–946.

Neubert, M. J., Carlson, D. S., Kacmar, K. M., Roberts, J. A., & Chonko, L. B. (2009). The virtuous influence of ethical leadership behavior: Evidence from the field. *Journal of Business Ethics, 90*(2), 157–170.

Nisar, T. M., Prabhakar, G., & Strakova, L. (2019). Social media information benefits, knowledge management and smart organizations. *Journal of Business Research, 94,* 264–272.

Seligman, M. E. (2002). Positive psychology, positive prevention, and positive therapy. *Handbook of positive psychology, 2*(2002), 3–12.

Sheikh, S., & Janoff-Bulman, R. (2010). The "shoulds" and "should nots" of moral emotions: A self-regulatory perspective on shame and guilt. *Personality and Social Psychology Bulletin, 36*(2), 213–224.

Sheldon, K. M., & King, L. (2001). Why positive psychology is necessary. *American Psychologist, 56*(3), 216.

Spillane, J. P., & Diamond, J. B. (2007). *Distributed leadership in practice.* New York: Teachers College, Columbia University.

Treviño, L. K., Weaver, G. R., & Reynolds, S. J. (2006). Behavioral ethics in organizations: A review. *Journal of Management, 32*(6), 951–990.

Tversky, A., & Kahneman, D. (1991). Loss aversion in riskless choice: A reference-dependent model. *The Quarterly Journal of Economics, 106*(4), 1039–1061.

Vaish, A., Grossmann, T., & Woodward, A. (2008). Not all emotions are created equal: The negativity bias in social-emotional development. *Psychological Bulletin, 134*(3), 383.

Williams, B. (1981). *Moral luck: Philosophical papers 1973–1980*. Cambridge: Cambridge University Press.

Zhu, D. H., & Westphal, J. D. (2011). Misperceiving the beliefs of others: How pluralistic ignorance contributes to the persistence of positive security analyst reactions to the adoption of stock repurchase plans. *Organization Science, 22*(4), 869–886.

Open Access This chapter is licensed under the terms of the Creative Commons Attribution 4.0 International License (http://creativecommons.org/licenses/by/4.0/), which permits use, sharing, adaptation, distribution and reproduction in any medium or format, as long as you give appropriate credit to the original author(s) and the source, provide a link to the Creative Commons licence and indicate if changes were made.

The images or other third party material in this chapter are included in the chapter's Creative Commons licence, unless indicated otherwise in a credit line to the material. If material is not included in the chapter's Creative Commons licence and your intended use is not permitted by statutory regulation or exceeds the permitted use, you will need to obtain permission directly from the copyright holder.

Index

A
Abductive inquiry, 11
Activism, 32
Amnesty International, 37
Anxiety, 76
Autonomy, 32, 55
Avoid-harm ethics, 62, 68, 76–79

B
Balanced leadership, 4, 62, 67, 73–75, 79
Big data, 7
Burnout, 76
Bystander effect, 75

C
Categorical imperative, 49
Code of conduct, 32

Competence dilemma, 34–36, 38, 39
Competition, 20, 36
Conflict, 22, 26, 27, 37, 53, 57, 76, 78
Consistency, 49–51

D
Decision-making, 6, 11, 20, 24, 26, 38, 44, 47, 52, 54, 56–60, 66, 68, 75, 79
Depression, 76
Diffusion of responsibility, 75
Digital transformation, 2, 11, 39, 76
Dilemma, 2–12, 18–40, 44–49, 53–62, 66, 67, 70–73, 75, 78, 79
Do-good ethics, 62, 68, 76, 78, 79
Duty ethics, 49, 51–53

Index

E

Economy, 3, 44, 57, 59, 61
Editor, 2, 4, 5, 31
Ethical analysis, 4, 24, 44, 45, 48, 49
Ethical debriefing, 45, 58–62
Ethical reasoning, 44
Ethical training, 11, 44, 54, 61
Ethics, 3–8, 11, 12, 18, 23, 33, 35, 44, 51, 58, 59, 61, 62, 66–79

F

Facebook, 2, 4, 5, 18–25, 28, 30–32, 34–36, 44–47, 49–52, 54, 56–58, 61, 69, 72–74
Fake news, 5, 32
False dilemma, 7, 9, 10, 25, 30, 35, 70
Framing, 38
Free speech, 32

G

Golden Rule, 6, 49
Greenpeace, 37

H

Harassment, 32
Honesty, 5, 23, 51, 52, 56
Horizontal leadership, 67, 68, 74, 75, 79

I

Instagram, 5, 18, 29, 66–69, 78
Integrity dilemma, 26–30, 33, 34, 38, 39, 71

J

Job satisfaction, 71
Journalist, 4, 5, 29, 48

K

Kahneman, D., 6, 24, 26, 44, 78
Kant, I., 49, 52
Knowledge hiding, 20
Knowledge sharing, 20

L

Law, 3, 44, 56, 59, 61
Leadership, 3, 4, 8, 11, 23, 55, 61, 62, 66–79
LinkedIn, 4, 5, 18, 20, 36
Loophole ethics, 33

M

Marketing, 7, 66
Moral dissonance, 18, 26
Morality, 3, 6–8, 44, 57, 59, 61
Moral luck, 25–27, 60, 61, 69

N

Nagel, T., 25, 60, 69
Narrative, 10, 66, 72

O

Overenget, E., 3, 44, 54–56

P

Personal integrity, 27, 28, 37
Pluralistic ignorance, 75
Positive organizational scholarship, 76

Principle of equality, 49–52, 58
Principle of publicity, 52–53, 57
Professional ethics, 35
Professional integrity, 27, 29, 37
Professionalism, 7, 34
Protection, 51, 67, 69

R

Rationalism, 7
Real dilemma, 9, 25
Reputation, 3, 44, 57, 59, 61
Resilience, 76
Responsibility, 3–5, 7, 22, 23, 33, 47, 66–76, 78, 79
Risk, 2, 22, 26, 27, 30, 35, 46, 49, 53, 57, 60, 68, 69, 76

S

Self-reflection, 9
Speech dilemma, 30–34, 38, 39, 45–49, 71

Stress, 76
System 1 and 2, 26, 44

T

Tempo dilemma, 23–26, 31, 34, 38, 39, 49, 60, 66
Trolling, 32
Twitter, 4, 5, 18, 20, 22–24, 28, 29, 32, 33, 35, 36, 61, 71–74

U

Utilitarian ethics, 51, 58

V

Vertical leadership, 67, 75, 79

W

Williams, B., 25, 60, 69

The manufacturer's authorised representative in the EU is Springer Nature Customer Service Centre GmbH, Europaplatz 3, 69115 Heidelberg, Germany. If you have any concerns regarding our products, please contact ProductSafety@springernature.com

Printed and bound by CPI Group (UK) Ltd, Croydon, CR0 4YY

25/03/2026

02078174-0001